REVI

REVELATION

meaningful mysteries for today

Terry Brooks

Harvestime

Published in the United Kingdom by:
Harvestime Services Ltd, 136 Hall Lane, Bradford
West Yorkshire BD4 7DG

First published by Harvestime
First printed June 1988

ISBN 0 947714 29 4

Typeset by: Grassroots Ltd, 364A Regents Park Road
London N3 2LJ
Printed and bound in the United Kingdom by:
Richard Clay Ltd, Bungay, Suffolk.

Introduction

'In form, symbolism, purpose and meaning, the book of Revelation is beautiful beyond description.

'Where in all of literature do we find anything that excels the majestic description of the Son of Man walking in the midst of the seven golden lampstands (1:12-20) or the vivid portrayal of the Christ, Faithful and True, going forth unto victory, seated upon a white horse, arrayed with a garment sprinkled with blood, followed by the armies of heaven (19:11-16)?'[1]

My desire in writing this book has been to make Revelation as readable as any other part of the New Testament.

Satan, with his usual craftiness and deceit, has assaulted the Bible on both flanks. He has attacked the first book of the Bible with the theory of evolution and the last book with many conflicting theories that major on defeat, confusion and fear.

I trust that, after reading this book, you will see Revelation as God intended.

> *'All Scripture is God-breathed and is useful for teaching, rebuking, correcting and training in righteousness, so that the man of God may be thoroughly equipped for every good work.'*
>
> (2 Timothy 3:16-17)

Terry Brooks
June 1988

---

1. William Hendriksen, *More Than Conquerors — An Interpretation of the Book of Revelation*, Baker Book House/Tyndale Press, 1939/1967

PLEASE NOTE

Unless otherwise stated,
all Bible references are to the book of Revelation

Contents

I

An Introduction to Revelation

1

Controversy and Comfort

The book of Revelation is probably the most misunderstood and controversial book of the Bible. But, seen in relation to God's ultimate intention, it should be the most exciting, encouraging and comforting book in the whole of Scripture.

1. The summary book of the Bible

As the last book, Revelation is a fitting climax to the entire Bible. It is the summary book of the whole of Scripture, presenting nothing that has not already been met elsewhere. All the major themes of the Bible are introduced in Genesis. Here, in Revelation, they are brought to fulness and finality:

> *'He told me, "Do not seal up the words of the prophecy of this book, because the time is near." '*
>
> (22:10)

It is fitting that the book of Revelation was written by the apostle John, who had a special gift for summarising truth. This gift is evident in his Gospel, where he picks and chooses from the teachings of Jesus to emphasise his theme of divine sonship:

> *'Jesus did many other miraculous signs in the presence of his disciples, which are not recorded in this book. But these are written that you may believe that Jesus is the Christ, the Son of God, and that by believing you may have life in his name.'*
>
> (John 20:30-31)

John's gift for summarising comes into full bloom in his book of Revelation.

2. The subject of the Bible

The opening words of Genesis unlock not only the book of Genesis but also the entire Bible:

> *'In the beginning God created the heavens and the earth.'*
>
> (Genesis 1:1)

Though the reference to 'heavens' is doubtless to the sun, moon and stars, perhaps there is also a hint of something more, for the Bible is essentially about two kingdoms, the kingdom of God (the heavens) and the kingdom of man (the earth). The two run like railway tracks through the entire Bible from Genesis to Revelation.

They may go under various names, but they are continuously in conflict. They are called: the two trees; the seed of the woman and the seed of the serpent; Cain and Abel; Abraham and Lot; Isaac and Ishmael; Moses and Pharaoh; David and Saul; Jerusalem and Babylon; Jesus and the Pharisees; spiritual and natural Israel; grace and law; the spirit and the flesh; the spiritual man and the natural man; and, finally, the Lamb and the red dragon.

In the book of Revelation we see the final conflict of these two kingdoms. We witness the ultimate defeat of Satan's kingdom and the establishment of the everlasting kingdom of the Lamb:

> *'The devil, who deceived them, was thrown into the lake of burning sulphur, where the beast and the false prophet had been thrown. They will be tormented day and night for ever and ever.'*
>
> (20:10)

> *'I saw the Holy City, the new Jerusalem, coming down out of heaven from God, prepared as a bride beautifully dressed for her husband. And I heard a loud voice from the throne saying, "Now the dwelling of God is with men, and he will live with them. They will be his people, and God himself will be with them and be their God." '*
>
> (21:2-3)

3. The title of the book

Since the book of Revelation is the summary book of the Bible, it is no surprise to find that its first verse provides us with an apt title for the whole Bible:

> *'The revelation of Jesus Christ, which God gave him to show his servants what must soon take place'.*
>
> (1:1)

What is the Bible but an unveiling of Jesus Christ? Our Lord Jesus is the subject of all Scripture:

> *'Beginning with Moses and all the Prophets, [Jesus] explained to them what was said in all the Scriptures concerning himself.'*
>
> (Luke 24:27)

> *'[Jesus] said to them, "This is what I told you while I was still with you: Everything must be fulfilled that is written about me in the Law of Moses, the Prophets and the Psalms." '*
>
> (Luke 24:44)

There is nothing in the Bible, from beginning to end, which does not concern the Lord Jesus. He is the Word (John 1:1-14). The Bible is the written Word, and Jesus is the living Word.

4. The light of the entire Bible

Revelation, therefore, being the last book, must be considered in the light of the rest of the Bible: all subjects and symbols must be interpreted according to their previous references. Obscurities in Revelation can only be explained by going back to earlier portions of Scripture.

The Old Testament, however, cannot be accurately applied to Revelation unless it is first filtered through and reinterpreted by the New Testament. It must be viewed in the light of Christ's first coming into history:

> *'The law is only a shadow of the good things that are coming — not the realities themselves.'*
>
> (Hebrews 10:1)

'In the past God spoke to our forefathers through the prophets at many times and in various ways, but in these last days he has spoken to us by his Son, whom he appointed heir of all things, and through whom he made the universe.'

(Hebrews 1:1-2)

Revelation is rooted not only in the surface soil of events occurring in John's generation but also in the subsoil of the rest of the Bible. We must interpret it in the light of both external events and the entire religious tradition of the Christian believers who lived when these visions were seen and recorded.

5. The first readers

Our starting point must always be: how did *the first readers* understand this book? We should make an earnest attempt to appreciate the conditions and circumstances out of which this prophecy arose.

a. The immediate purpose

The book's immediate purpose is to comfort and strengthen the wavering hearts of persecuted believers in the first century AD. It was addressed to real, live people:

'John, To the seven churches in the province of Asia: Grace and peace to you from him who is, and who was, and who is to come, and from the seven spirits before his throne, and from Jesus Christ, who is the faithful witness, the firstborn from the dead, and the ruler of the kings of the earth.'

(1:4-5)

We must therefore permit the contemporary circumstances to shed light on the book's symbols and visions.

b. Not primarily future

These first-century believers were not interested so much in the great events of future centuries as in the struggle between light and darkness, the church and the world, Christ and the dragon, truth and error, being waged in their own time. This book is an answer to the crying needs of these persecuted believers:

> *'Do not be afraid of what you are about to suffer. I tell you, the devil will put some of you in prison to test you, and you will suffer persecution for ten days. Be faithful, even to the point of death, and I will give you the crown of life.'*
>
> (2:10)

6. Spans the entire church age

This does not mean that John was limited to matters within his own historical horizon. This book spans the entire church age and is intended for us as well as for the believers of the first century:

> *'Write, therefore, what you have seen, what is now and what will take place later.'*
>
> (1:19)

7. The nature of the book: a drama

Revelation is best described as a drama. There are characters, changing scenes and action. The title of the drama is *The Unveiling* (bringing to light):

> *'The revelation [literally, unveiling] of Jesus Christ, which God gave him to show his servants what must soon take place.'*
>
> (1:1)

Basically this is a moving-picture book. Here we have the last dramatic scene of a long and difficult criminal case finally unravelled. We are presented with clues, exhibits, records, witnesses, culprits, jury and judge.

The lid is taken off everything — heaven, hell, the abyss, the dead, demons, Satan and all his subordinates. The only things not revealed are the sins of the saints, which have been covered (atoned for) by the blood of the Lamb.

> *'I saw a Lamb, looking as if it had been slain, standing in the centre of the throne, encircled by the four living creatures and the elders. He had seven horns and seven eyes, which are the seven spirits of God sent out into all the earth. He came and took the scroll from the right hand of him who sat on the throne.'*
>
> (5:6-7)

The unveiling is not only *of* Jesus Christ but *by* Jesus Christ — the dominant figure in the drama.

a. Unravelling mysteries

He alone is capable of unravelling the age-long, universal mysteries of injustice, oppression, deception, suffering and death:

> *'One of the elders said to me, "Do not weep! See, the Lion of the tribe of Judah, the Root of David, has triumphed. He is able to open the scroll and its seven seals." '*
>
> (5:5)

b. Access to secrets

He alone has access to the secrets of the soul, sea, sky, soil:

> *'I know your deeds.'*
>
> (2:2)

> *'I know your afflictions.'*
>
> (2:9)

> *'I know where you live.'*
>
> (2:13)

c. Producing witnesses

He alone has the power to produce all of the witnesses together in court. It is he who brings all things to their final judgment, verdict and execution:

> *'When I saw him, I fell at his feet as though dead. Then he placed his right hand on me and said: "Do not be afraid. I am the First and the Last. I am the Living One; I was dead, and behold I am alive for ever and ever! And I hold the keys of death and Hades."'*
>
> (1:17-18)

8. The central fact of the book

All this, however, is only background. The central fact is the revelation of Jesus Christ himself. The unveiling of the Lord Jesus in all his glory is the Father's express purpose and pleasure, so that his Son might be highly exalted.

> *'God exalted him to the highest place and gave him the name that is above every name, that at the name of Jesus every knee should bow, in heaven and on earth and under the earth, and every tongue confess that Jesus Christ is Lord, to the glory of God the Father.'*
>
> (Philippians 2:9-11)

a. Christ, the goal of all history

Jesus Christ is the goal of all history and the pinnacle of all prophecy. The burden of Scripture is the supreme glory of Christ (the Word). He is the hope of creation and the desire of all nations.

> *'The creation was subjected to frustration, not by its own choice, but by the will of the one who subjected it, in hope that the creation itself will be liberated from its bondage to decay and brought into the glorious freedom of the children of God.'*
>
> (Romans 8:20-21)

b. Not chaos, but Christ

History is not moving towards chaos, but towards Christ. The first coming of Christ divided history; the second coming will conclude it. Humankind's history, to be rightly understood, must be Christocentric (Christ-centred), otherwise it will be eccentric (off-centre).

> *'He is the image of the invisible God, the firstborn over all creation. For by him all things were created: things in heaven and on earth, visible and invisible, whether thrones or powers or rulers or authorities; all things were created by him and for him. He is before all things, and in him all things hold together. And he is the head of the body, the church; he is the beginning and the firstborn from among the dead, so that in everything he might have the supremacy.'*
>
> (Colossians 1:15-18)

9. The hope of our calling

It is essential to interpret the book of Revelation properly because it contains the hope for our future. The New Testament gives us practical reasons for knowing and understanding this hope:

> *'In your hearts set apart Christ as Lord. Always be prepared to give an answer to everyone who asks you to give the reason for the hope that you have. But do this with gentleness and respect, keeping a clear conscience, so that those who speak maliciously against your good behaviour in Christ may be ashamed of their slander.'*
>
> (1 Peter 3:15-16)

How can we be prepared to give reasons for our hope if we do not know or understand it?

a. Peace of mind

Peace of mind is a direct result of having a secure hope:

> *'Since we belong to the day, let us be self-controlled, putting on faith and love as a breastplate, and the hope of salvation as a helmet.'*
>
> (1 Thessalonians 5:8)

A helmet cushions a blow on the head, so that we do not lose consciousness. Our hope keeps our mind at peace so that we do not lose our sense of direction and calling for our lives.

b. An anchor for the soul

The troubled events of the times in which we live can produce feelings of instability and insecurity. But our hope acts as an anchor for our emotions so that we are not at the mercy of these ever-changing currents of life:

> *'God did this so that, by two unchangeable things in which it is impossible for God to lie, we who have fled to take hold of the hope offered to us may be greatly encouraged. We have this hope as an anchor for the soul, firm and secure. It enters the inner sanctuary behind the curtain, where Jesus, who went before us, has entered on our behalf. He has become a high priest for ever, in the order of Melchizedek.'*
>
> (Hebrews 6:18-20)

The chain for this anchor is faith. Faith is the means of laying hold of the anchor of hope which is in Christ:

> *'Faith is being sure of what we hope for and certain of what we do not see.'*
>
> (Hebrews 11:1)

c. Purity of behaviour

Purity of behaviour is a clear product of a secure hope:

> *'Dear friends, now we are children of God, and what we will be has not yet been made known. But we know that when he appears, we shall be like him, for we shall see him as he is. Everyone who has this hope in him purifies himself, just as he is pure.'*
>
> (1 John 3:2-3)

Peace of mind and stability of character must be accompanied by behaviour that is free of hypocrisy. Our hope produces both purity of motive (inward) and integrity of behaviour (outward).

d. Physical health and vitality

Stress is one of today's leading causes of illness. Knowing the hope of the future can eliminate much of our daily stress and thus bring health to our bodies.

> *'If the Spirit of him who raised Jesus from the dead is living in you, he who raised Christ from the dead will also give life to your mortal bodies through his Spirit, who lives in you.'*
>
> (Romans 8:11)

One day we will have glorified bodies that will be altogether superior to our present perishable ones. In the meantime we can live and enjoy health in our mortal bodies by appropriating our hope.

e. Prayer sensitivity and effectiveness

Our hope also guides us in prayer by enabling us to be sensitive to the Spirit's direction:

> *'In this hope we were saved. But hope that is seen is no hope at all. Who hopes for what he already has? But if we hope for what we do not yet have, we wait for it patiently. In the same way, the Spirit helps us in our weakness. We do not know what we ought to pray for, but the Spirit himself intercedes for us with groans that words cannot express.'*
>
> (Romans 8:24-26)

Study questions on Chapter 1: Controversy and Comfort

1. Why do we need to know about our hope?

2. In what ways is Revelation meant for the first century church? In what ways is it meant for us today?

3. How is this book both an unveiling *of* Jesus and an unveiling *by* Jesus?

4. Find examples of the two 'kingdoms' in Revelation. Make a list of their opposite attributes and names.

True or False

1. The book of Revelation introduces new visions and symbols not found anywhere else in the Bible.

2. Revelation displays the final conflict between the kingdom of Satan and the kingdom of God.

3. Old Testament symbols can be applied directly to Revelation.

4. The book of Revelation is primarily intended as a message of comfort and hope.

5. Revelation is pertinent to our twentieth-century generation only, since we are in the last days.

6. Revelation is best described as a drama.

7. The centre of all history is Jesus Christ.

8. History is moving towards a chaotic end which no-one can do anything about.

9. When our hope is fixed on Jesus our motives and behaviour will become pure.

10. Revelation is a summary of the whole Bible.

11. Jesus Christ, the subject of Revelation, is also the subject of the whole Bible.

True or False

1.F 2.T 3.F 4.T 5.F 6.T 7.T 8.F 9.T 10.T 11.T

2

Visions and Symbols

1. A book of visions

Visions provide the central focus of Revelation: 'Then I saw . . . .' But visions are not an end in themselves; each one must have an outworking if it is to be effective in its purpose. The rest of the book, therefore, is concerned with the outworking of the visions:

> *'Blessed (happy, to be envied) is the man who reads aloud [in the assemblies] the word of this prophecy; and blessed (happy, to be envied) are those who hear [it read] and who keep themselves true to the things which are written in it — heeding them and laying them to heart — for the time [for them to be fulfilled] is near.'*
>
> (1:3 Amplified Bible)

> *'Behold, I am coming soon! Blessed is he who keeps the words of the prophecy in this book.'*
>
> (22:7)

a. In the Spirit

In order to interpret the visions properly, we must view them as John did.

> *'On the Lord's Day I was in the Spirit.'*
>
> (1:10)

> *'I was in the Spirit, and there before me was a throne in heaven with someone sitting on it.'*
>
> (4:2)

> *'The angel carried me away in the Spirit into a desert.'*
>
> (17:3)

> *'[An angel] carried me away in the Spirit to a mountain great and high, and showed me the Holy City, Jerusalem, coming down out of heaven from God.'*
>
> (21:10)

If we, too, are not 'in the Spirit' when we examine the visions and symbols, we will tend to give them an over-literal interpretation.

b. For the universal church

The visions in Revelation are not just for John or a select number of Christians of his era but for the church in every age and place:

> *' "I, Jesus, have sent my angel to give you this testimony for the churches. I am the Root and the Offspring of David, and the bright Morning Star." The Spirit and the bride say, "Come!" And let him who hears say, "Come!" Whoever is thirsty, let him come; and whoever wishes, let him take the free gift of the water of life.'*
>
> (22:16-17)

c. People perish without vision

Without vision people perish. The whole plan and course of salvation is based on vision. Every stream of action should have as its source vision from the throne itself:

> *'Where there is no vision [no redemptive revelations of God], the people perish; but he who keeps the law [of God, which includes that of man], blessed, happy, fortunate [and enviable] is he.'*
>
> (Proverbs 29:18 Amplified Bible)

What is your vision of God and of his purpose for your life? He is not mean and punishing or a Sunday-morning-only God. He is not a Santa Claus or a remote, theological God. Your view of God will determine how you live your Christian life. The proper concept of God was made known to us through Jesus Christ, who revealed him as our *Father:*

> *'My Father, who has given them to me, is greater than all; no-one can snatch them out of my Father's hand. I and the Father are one.'*
>
> (John 10:29-30)

By understanding the visions in Revelation, we can discover the purpose for our lives in God's plan for the church.

2. A book of symbols

Revelation is a book of symbols expressing heavenly realities, and it must always be treated as such:

> *'The revelation of Jesus Christ, which God gave him to show his servants — things which must shortly take place. And he sent and signified it by his angel to his servant John.'*
>
> (1:1 RAV)

With the word 'sign-ified' (and its Greek original), John lets us know early in the book that he will be using a symbolic, poetic language to express these heavenly realities:

> *'The mystery of the seven stars that you saw in my right hand and of the seven golden lampstands is this: The seven stars are the angels of the seven churches, and the seven lampstands are the seven churches.'*
>
> (1:20)

In simple terms, Revelation is written in a language employing Old Testament references. Those who lack familiarity with the Old Testament's content and language, therefore, will be unable to understand these references.

a. Old Testament symbols

Symbols are used in every book of the Old Testament, and especially in the books of prophecy such as Daniel. References abound to the tree of life, cherubim, the tabernacle, the ark of the covenant, altars, a brazen serpent and many other symbols. The Old Testament became a type and illustration of spiritual realities which came into being with the coming of Christ:

> *'Since the Law has merely a rude outline (foreshadowing) of the good things to come, instead of fully expressing those things, it can never by offering the same sacrifices continually year after year make perfect those who approach [its altars].'*
>
> (Hebrews 10:1 Amplified Bible)

> *'These things happened to them as examples and were written down as warnings for us, on whom the fulfilment of the ages has come.'*
>
> (1 Corinthians 10:11)

b. Modern usage of symbols

We ourselves frequently use symbols. Think of: the national flag; the White House; the iron curtain; a horseshoe; a black cat; Uncle Sam; a rabbit's foot; a broken mirror; a red carpet; a four-leaf clover; Cupid. Of what are they symbolic?

c. The distinction between principle and detail

Revelation consists of moving pictures, spiritual cartoons or changing scenes which are full of action. To dissect these symbols is to risk losing their unity. The details of a vision should be interpreted in harmony with its central thought, in the same way as we would interpret a parable like the Good Samaritan.

3. Two kinds of symbols

In dealing with symbols we should always ask two questions:

- ☐ What is the overall picture?
- ☐ What is its predominant idea or principle?

There are two kinds of symbols in the book of Revelation:

a. A specific event

Some symbols usually refer to a specific event. These symbols describe the beginning or end of divine activity:

> *'Another angel came out of the temple and called in a loud voice to him who was sitting on the cloud, "Take your sickle and reap, because the time to reap has come, for the harvest of the earth is ripe." '*
>
> (14:15)

b. A series of events

Other symbols seem to refer to a whole series of happenings, to broad principles of human and satanic conduct and divine moral government which operate between Christ's first and second comings. They refer to the kind of thing that happens repeatedly — persecution, for example — so that the book of Revelation is always up to date.

The seals, trumpets, bowls and similar pictures come in this category. They refer not to specific events or details of history but to principles operating throughout the history of the world, especially throughout this entire church age:

> *'[They] sang the song of Moses the servant of God and the song of the Lamb: "Great and marvellous are your deeds, Lord God Almighty. Just and true are your ways, King of the ages. Who will not fear you, O Lord, and bring glory to your name? For you alone are holy. All nations will come and worship before you, for your righteous acts have been revealed." '*
>
> (15:3-4)

4. Numbers and their significance

John conveys a great deal by his use of numbers, especially the numbers four, seven, ten and twelve and their multiples.

a. Not mathematics

We think of numbers as mathematics but, to the Jews, numbers often conveyed concepts and ideas.

So we should not look for mathematical exactitude in John's use of numbers, but rather the main idea he is seeking to convey. It is another aspect of Revelation's symbolism. John gives us an example when he writes:

> *'If anyone has insight, let him calculate the number of the beast, for it is man's number. His number is 666.'*
>
> (13:18)

b. Be consistent

It is obviously foolish to try visualising a physical beast with ten horns or seven heads, and yet some Christians are looking for a literal 144,000 from the twelve tribes, as well as a literal thousand-year millenium.

We need to be consistent in our numerical interpretation and not jump back and forth from symbolism to literalism. We will return to the meaning and use of these symbolic numbers later.

c. General agreement

Scholars from each of the classical schools of interpretation of Revelation are generally agreed on the meaning of the symbols and numbers. The conflict in their interpretations surrounds the timescale of these events.

5. Prejudices and preconceptions

Every reader or interpreter brings certain prejudices with him to the study of this book. In order to discover its truth, it is necessary, though difficult, to divorce ourselves from any rigid preconceptions gained by our having been schooled in any one method of interpretation. We have the Holy Spirit to guide us:

> *'As for you, the anointing you received from him remains in you, and you do not need anyone to teach you. But as his anointing teaches you about all things and as that anointing is real, not counterfeit — just as it has taught you, remain in him.'*
>
> (1 John 2:27)

Most of us have formed our opinions about Revelation from what we have read or heard from the 'experts'. Unfortunately, we have neither taken the time nor exerted the discipline necessary to study the book on our own, asking God to reveal his truths to us.

Do not absorb unquestioningly the interpretation in this study. Submit it to the 'Berean test':

> *'The Bereans were of more noble character than the Thessalonians, for they received the message with great eagerness and examined the Scriptures every day to see if what Paul said was true.'*
>
> (Acts 17:11)

6. Four methods of interpretation

There are four classical methods of interpreting the book of Revelation. Almost all the material written on it could be slotted into one of these categories. Each of the four methods contains an element of truth, though none possesses the whole truth. Any one interpretation by itself is seriously lacking in balance.

a. The preterist view (contemporary-historical)

According to this view, there is no prophetic element in the book at all. Revelation is simply a sketch of conditions in the Roman Empire in the first century and nothing more than an interpretation of the events of the generation in which it was written. It was written to encourage the churches of that generation only.

In support of this view, its proponents cite the epistle-format of the book:

> *'John, To the seven churches in the province of Asia: Grace and peace to you from him who is, and who was, and who is to come, and from the seven spirits before his throne, and from Jesus Christ, who is the faithful witness, the firstborn from the dead, and the ruler of the kings of the earth.'*
>
> (1:4-5)

b. The historicist view (continuous-historical)

According to this view, Revelation is a symbolic presentation of the events of church history from the close of the first century to the end of time.

It is difficult to take this view seriously for one is constantly confronted with the dilemma of how to reconcile a far-fetched spiritualisation with a chain of literal, historical events.

c. The idealist view (symbolic, spiritual or poetic)

Expositors of this school of thought see the book as relevant to every generation from the time it was written, and to no generation in particular. It is a pictorial presentation of ideas, principles and concepts occurring repeatedly in the history of humankind.

This method avoids the problem of trying to find any historical fulfilment of the symbols of Revelation. Its supporters see only a symbolic portrayal of the spiritual, cosmic conflict between the kingdom of God and the powers of evil.

d. The futurist view

This method interprets Revelation largely as a prophecy, in symbolic terms, of future events leading up to and accompanying the end of the world. The futurist view has taken two forms which we may call the *extreme* and *moderate* futurist views. The former is also known as dispensationalism.

i. Extreme (dispensationalist) futurism

The letters to the seven churches in Revelation 2 and 3 are seen as seven successive ages of church history symbolically portrayed. The character of each of the seven churches depicts the chief characteristics of the relevant period of church history, the last one being a period of decline and apostasy (Laodicea).

The 'rapture' of John (Revelation 4) is thought to symbolise the rapture of the church before the great tribulation occurs:

> *'I looked, and there before me was a door standing open in heaven. And the voice I had first heard speaking to me like a trumpet said, "Come up here, and I will show you what must take place after this."'*
>
> (4:1)

In the dispensational view God's *earthly* people are the Jews of Israel — restored to Jerusalem, protected by a divine sealing (7:1-8) and with a rebuilt temple (11:1-3) — who suffer the wrath of the antichrist. The Christian church, by contrast, are God's *heavenly* people, no longer on the earth, for they have been caught up in the air to be with the Lord (4:1; 1 Thessalonians 4:16-17).

ii. Moderate futurism

The moderate futurist view finds no reason to distinguish so sharply between Israel and the Christian church. The people of God who face fearful persecution are the church. Supporters of this view find no reason to see in the seven letters to the churches a forecast of seven ages of church history. They do, however, agree with the dispensationalist that the primary purpose of the book is to describe the consummation of God's redemptive purpose at the end of the age. To summarise the four perspectives:

1. The *preterist* sees no prophetic element in the book. It is merely an interpretation of the events of the generation in which it was written.

2. The *historicist* views the book as a symbolic outline of church and world history from the birth of Jesus to the end of the age.

3. The *idealist* sees it as being relevant to every generation but to no generation in particular. It is a pictorial representation of ideas occurring repeatedly in the history of man.

4. The *futurist* sees the book's message and interpretation as applicable only to the final generation of history.

7. The Old Testament prophetic perspective

There is one characteristic of Old Testament prophecy which is also characteristic of Revelation — one which solves the problem of time and relevance. The Old Testament prophets seem to have had two views in their prophetic perspective: first, the events of the present and immediate future; and, second, the ultimate consummation. Their prophecies had a short-term fulfilment and also a much broader relevance. These two are held in dynamic tension, often without chronological distinction.

The main purpose of prophecy is not to give a programme or chart of the future but to let the light of the ultimate consummation fall on the present:

> '*We have the word of the prophets made more certain, and you will do well to pay attention to it, as to a light shining in a dark place, until the day dawns and the morning star rises in your hearts.*'
>
> (2 Peter 1:19)

As indicated previously, any one method of interpretation is lacking in balance, for none does justice to the whole truth. The best approach is to study the book in the terms John used to describe it. This we will do in the remainder of this book.

Study questions on Chapter 2: Visions and Symbols

1. 'Without vision all initiative is stifled.' Consider the role of vision in our lives as Christians.

2. What are the advantages and disadvantages of each of the methods of interpretation? Why is it important to balance them against each other?

3. Why could it be dangerous or foolish to interpret symbolic statements literally? In what ways do we tend to do exactly that today?

4. Trace three of the symbols in Revelation back to their Old Testament origins.

5. Search the Old Testament for parallels to the images in Revelation 1:20. Start by looking at Daniel 7 — 12.

True or False

1. Events in Revelation should be approached from the point of view that John saw them: 'in the Spirit'.

2. Every stream of action should have as its source vision from God.

3. John's symbols should be taken literally when it seems plausible.

4. Visions and symbols were used throughout the Old Testament.

5. It is important to decipher every detail of a symbolic message in order to grasp the central principle.

6. Symbols can refer to a specific event or to a series of events.

7. The Jews incorporated numbers into their Scriptures because of their mathematical significance.

8. Each reader who wants to discover the truth of Revelation must divorce himself of any rigid preconceptions about methods of interpretation.

9. The four methods of interpreting Revelation are all valid and perfectly acceptable.

10. The main purpose of prophecy is simply to predict future events.

True or False

1.T 2.T 3.F 4.T 5.F 6.T 7.F 8.T 9.F 10.F

3

John's Approach

1. The best approach

The best approach to the study of the book of Revelation is in the terms used by John himself. He considered it as:

a. An apocalypse

The word 'apocalypse' simply means an 'unveiling' (not a hiding) or 'revelation' of what has been hidden (the mystery). It isn't meant to introduce us to additional mysteries but rather to unveil a message which is as essential to the church of our own time as it was to the seven churches to whom John wrote specifically:

> *'The revelation [apocalypse] of Jesus Christ, which God gave him to show his servants what must soon take place.'*
>
> (1:1)

It is an unfolding, from a divine perspective, of the meaning of events in our visible world (the earth). These events illustrate the cosmic conflict between the Lamb and Satan which is going on in the invisible world (the heavens).

b. A prophecy

John views Revelation as a book of prophecy, carrying the same weight as the Old Testament books of prophecy:

> *'Blessed is the one who reads the words of this prophecy, and blessed are those who hear it and take to heart what is written in it, because the time is near.'*
>
> (1:3)

'If anyone takes words away from this book of prophecy, God will take away from him his share in the tree of life and in the holy city, which are described in this book.'

(22:19)

The writer implies that he himself is a prophet:

'He said to me, "Do not do it! I am a fellow-servant with you and with your brothers the prophets and of all who keep the words of this book. Worship God!" '

(22:9)

All prophets primarily addressed their contemporaries and the situation of their time, but they were always looking forward to a future consummation. The book, therefore, must be interpreted as having application to the churches in John's generation as well as having a future fulfilment in later generations.

c. A pastoral letter

In the same way that Paul, in introducing his letters, always stated to whom his letter was addressed, John tells us to whom Revelation is written:

'John, To the seven churches in the province of Asia: Grace and peace to you from him who is, and who was, and who is to come, and from the seven spirits before his throne.'

(1:4)

Being a pastoral letter (epistle), it focuses on some of the issues which were current problems in the churches, as well as on the political context of their times as part of the Roman Empire.

2. The purpose of the book

Generally, the purpose of the book of Revelation is *to comfort the churches in their struggle against the forces of evil.* It is full of hope and comfort for the persecuted and suffering Christians.

To them is given the assurance that:

a. Their tears and their suffering are seen by God

'The Lamb at the centre of the throne will be their shepherd; he will lead them to springs of living water. And God will wipe away every tear from their eyes.'

(7:17)

b. Their prayers are influential in world affairs

'Another angel, who had a golden censer, came and stood at the altar. He was given much incense to offer, with the prayers of all the saints, on the golden altar before the throne. The smoke of the incense, together with the prayers of the saints, went up before God from the angel's hand.'

(8:3-4)

c. Their final victory is assured

'I saw what looked like a sea of glass mixed with fire and, standing beside the sea, those who had been victorious over the beast and his image and over the number of his name. They held harps given them by God and sang the song of Moses the servant of God and the song of the Lamb.'

(15:2-3)

d. Their blood will be avenged

'True and just are his judgments. He has condemned the great prostitute who corrupted the earth by her adulteries. He has avenged on her the blood of his servants.'

(19:2)

e. Their Lord lives and reigns for ever and ever

He is governing the world in the interests of his church:

'One of the four living creatures gave to the seven angels seven golden bowls filled with the wrath of God, who lives for ever and ever. And the temple was filled with smoke from the glory of God and from his power, and no-one could enter the temple until the seven plagues of the seven angels were completed.'

(15:7-8)

f. Their Christ is coming again

He is coming to take his people to himself at the 'marriage supper of the Lamb', and to live with them for ever in a regenerated universe:

' "Let us rejoice and be glad and give him glory! For the wedding of the Lamb has come, and his bride has made herself ready. Fine linen, bright and clean, was given her to wear." (Fine linen stands for the righteous acts of the saints.) Then the angel said to me, "Write: 'Blessed are those who are invited to the wedding supper of the Lamb!' " And he added, "These are the true words of God." '

(19:7-9)

The assurances given to these first-century Christians should be just as comforting to Christians of every generation.

3. The theme of the book

The theme of the book is *the victory of Christ and of his church over the dragon (Satan) and his helpers*. Revelation is meant to show us that things aren't what they seem to be in the visible world. For example, the beast that comes up out of the abyss seems at first to be victorious:

'When they have finished their testimony, the beast that comes up from the Abyss will attack them, and overpower and kill them.'

(11:7)

Yet, in reality it is the believer who triumphs:

> *'After the three and half days a breath of life from God entered them, and they stood on their feet, and terror struck those who saw them.'*
>
> (11:11)

a. The conquering Lion

Throughout the prophecies of this book, Christ is pictured as the victor and the conqueror. He conquers death, Hades, the dragon, the beast, the false prophet and the people who worship the beast. Because he is victorious, we also triumph, even when outwardly we seem to be defeated.

b. The overcoming Lamb

In short, the theme of the book is stated most gloriously and completely in these words:

> *'They will make war against the Lamb, but the Lamb will overcome them because he is Lord of lords and King of kings — and with him will be his called, chosen and faithful followers.'*
>
> (17:14)

4. Views of history

There are two prevailing views of history:

a. Apocalyptic

This view holds that, left to itself, the world would become so evil that God would need to break into it from outside, unaided by man, in order to bring about his purposes and goals.

b. Prophetic

This view holds that God and his people may co-operate, working together for the accomplishment of his purposes in this age.

c. John's view

John combines these views. Revelation is an apocalyptic book of the same order as Daniel. It is also as prophetic a book as the prophetic writings of the Old Testament. John sees:

☐ This age already entered by God

This age has already been invaded by God in the birth of Jesus. The Word has become flesh. Jesus has brought the life of the age to come in his own person and being:

> *'[The woman] gave birth to a son, a male child, who will rule all the nations with an iron sceptre. And her child was snatched up to God and to his throne.'*
>
> (12:5)

☐ Christians living in both ages simultaneously

We who are the people of God are viewed by John as living simultaneously in both this age and the age to come. We are tomorrow's people living today. The values, nature and government of these two ages or worlds are opposite, and in opposition to one another:

> *'Do not love the world or anything in the world. If anyone loves the world, the love of the Father is not in him. For everything in the world — the cravings of sinful man, the lust of his eyes and and the boasting of what he has and does — comes not from the Father but from the world. The world and its desires pass away, but the man who does the will of God lives for ever.'*
>
> (1 John 2:15-17)

It is with this background knowledge of John's generation and of his attitude to the Christian life, then, that we approach an interpretation of the book of Revelation.

5. The two main divisions

a. The world persecutes the church

In the first group of visions (Revelation 1 — 11), we see the struggle among men, that is, between believers and unbelievers. The world attacks the church, but the church is avenged, protected and victorious:

> *'When he opened the fifth seal, I saw under the altar the souls of those who had been slain because of the word of God and the testimony they had maintained. They called out in a loud voice, "How long, Sovereign Lord, holy and true, until you judge the inhabitants of the earth and avenge our blood?"'*
>
> (6:9-10)

b. The dragon wages war with the Lamb

In the second group of visions (Revelation 12 — 22), we are shown that this struggle on earth takes place against an important background. It is merely the outward manifestation of something more fundamental: the devil's attack on the male child (Jesus).

i. The dragon attacks the church

The dragon first attacks the Lamb. Being repulsed, he directs all his fury against the church. Satan employs the two beasts and the great prostitute as his helpers.

> *'The dragon was enraged at the woman and went off to make war against the rest of her offspring — those who obey God's commandments and hold to the testimony of Jesus.'*
>
> (12:17)

But, in the end, all these enemies of the church are inevitably defeated.

ii. An intensifying spiritual conflict

Within this second group of visions (chapters 12 to 22), there are sections which parallel each other; yet, when viewed collectively, they present a continuing story. The dragon, the beasts, the prostitute (note the order) assail the church. The prostitute, the beasts, the dragon (again, note the order) are overthrown. The book of Revelation therefore reveals a progression in depth or intensity of spiritual conflict.

> *'The devil, who deceived them, was thrown into the lake of burning sulphur, where the beast and the false prophet had been thrown. They will be tormented day and night for ever and ever.'*
>
> (20:10)

6. The unity of the book

Even though we can now easily see the divisions of the book, it is the *unity* of the book that should be emphasised. We must always be aware of the very close relationship between all the parts.

A careful reading of Revelation makes it clear that the book consists of several sections, as follows:

- ☐ Christ and the seven churches (chapters 1 — 3)
- ☐ The Lamb and the seven-sealed scroll (4 — 7)
- ☐ The seven trumpets (8 — 11)
- ☐ The battle (12 — 14)
- ☐ The seven bowls of wrath (15 — 16)
- ☐ The fall of Babylon and Satan (17 — 20)
- ☐ Everything made new (21 — 22)

Revelation doesn't give us a chronological order of events from chapters 1 to 22. *Each* of the sections describes this present age from the first to the second coming of Christ, and brings us right up to the end of the world as we know it. This same period of time is viewed from one aspect, then from another, as each section succeeds the ones before it.

And, of course, the teachings of these seven sections, which reveal such a glorious unity and gradual blossoming of thought, agree with the rest of the Bible, as we shall see.

7. A closer look at each section

It is recommended that you now read each section. Other scriptures and comments are provided to help you understand each one. In particular, verses from other parts of the Bible are provided to show that the message of Revelation is in harmony with Scripture as a whole.

But to begin with, we could say that the whole book of Revelation could be summed up in the words of Jesus in a single verse from John's Gospel:

> *'I have told you these things, so that in me you may have peace. In this world you will have trouble. But take heart! I have overcome the world.'*
>
> (John 16:33)

Now let us look at each section separately, noticing in particular how each one brings us right up to the end of the world. Read chapters 1 to 3.

a. Christ and the seven churches

At the conclusion of each of the seven letters we are given a glimpse into the age after the final judgment. The closing verses of this section show that the overcomers will rule and reign with their King for eternity:

> *'To him who overcomes, I will give the right to sit with me on my throne, just as I overcame and sat down with my Father on his throne.'*
>
> (3:21)

The church always functions as a light-bearer, shining in the midst of the darkness of this world, but assured of the constant presence of their Lord and Saviour:

> *'You are the light of the world. A city on a hill cannot be hidden. Neither do people light a lamp and put it under a bowl. Instead they put it on its stand, and it gives light to everyone in the house. In the same way, let your light shine before men, that they may see your good deeds and praise your Father in heaven.'*
>
> (Matthew 5:14-16)

> *'Surely I am with you always, to the very end of the age.'*
>
> (Matthew 28:20)

Now read chapters 4 to 7.

b. The Lamb and the seven-sealed scroll

Observe the impression of the day of God's wrath on the unbelievers:

> *'The kings of the earth, the princes, the generals, the rich, the mighty, and every slave and every free man hid in caves and among the rocks of the mountains. They called to the mountains and the rocks, "Fall on us and hide us from the face of him who sits on the throne and from the wrath of the Lamb! For the great day of their wrath has come, and who can stand?"'*
>
> (6:15-17)

Notice that, together with the opening of the seven seals, we again receive a picture of the end of this age:

> *'These are they who have come out of the great tribulation; they have washed their robes and made them white in the blood of the Lamb. Therefore, they are before the throne of God and serve him day and night in his temple; and he who sits on the throne will spread his tent over them. Never again will they hunger; never again will they thirst. The sun will not beat upon them, nor any scorching heat.'*
>
> (7:14-16)

The church shines because Christ dwells in it, and consequently it is persecuted by the world. In this section we see the Lamb on the throne working all things together for the good of his kingdom.

> *'I have told you these things, so that in me you may have peace. In this world you will have trouble. But take heart! I have overcome the world.'*
>
> (John 16:33)

> *'[Jesus] is the image of the invisible God, the firstborn over all creation. For by him all things were created: things in heaven and on earth, visible and invisible, whether thrones or powers or rulers or authorities; all things were created by him and for him. He is*

> *before all things, and in him all things hold together. And he is the head of the body, the church; he is the beginning and the firstborn from among the dead, so that in everything he might have the supremacy.'*
>
> (Colossians 1:15-18)

Now read chapters 8 to 11.

c. The seven trumpets

With the blowing of the seventh trumpet, we again have a picture of the end of the age, with a clear reference to the final judgment:

> *'The kingdom of the world has become the kingdom of our Lord and of his Christ, and he will reign for ever and ever.'*
>
> (11:15)

> *'The nations were angry; and your wrath has come. The time has come for judging the dead, and for rewarding your servants the prophets and your saints and those who reverence your name, both small and great — and for destroying those who destroy the earth.'*
>
> (11:18)

Once again, divine judgments of every description fall upon the world, while the church is victorious:

> *'Will not God bring about justice for his chosen ones, who cry out to him day and night? Will he keep putting them off? I tell you, he will see that they get justice, and quickly. However, when the Son of Man comes, will he find faith on the earth?'*
>
> (Luke 18:7-8)

Now read chapters 12 to 14.

d. The battle

This section closes with a stirring description of Christ's second coming in judgment:

'Another angel came out of the temple and called in a loud voice to him who was sitting on the cloud, "Take your sickle and reap, because the time to reap has come, for the harvest of the earth is ripe." So he who was seated on the cloud swung his sickle over the earth, and the earth was harvested.'

(14:15-16)

This struggle between the church and the world always reveals an even deeper conflict between Christ and Satan. Satan repeatedly employs the allies mentioned in this section.

'I will put enmity between you and the woman, and between your offspring and hers; he will crush your head, and you will strike his heel.'

(Genesis 3:15)

Now read chapters 15 and 16.

e. The seven bowls of wrath

Revelation 15 and 16 describe the bowls of wrath. Here is a clear reference to the events that will take place in connection with the final judgment:

'They gathered the kings together to the place that in Hebrew is called Armageddon. The seventh angel poured out his bowl into the air, and out of the temple came a loud voice from the throne, saying, "It is done!" . . . The great city split into three parts, and the cities of the nations collapsed. God remembered Babylon the Great and gave her the cup filled with the wine of the fury of his wrath.'

(16:16-19)

The enemies of the Lamb always, and especially on the day of judgment, go down in defeat. Our victory is assured!

'Because of your stubbornness and your unrepentant heart, you are storing up wrath against yourself for the day of God's wrath, when his righteous judgment will be revealed. God "will give to each person according to what he has done". To those who by persistence in doing good seek glory, honour and

> *immortality, he will give eternal life. But for those who are self-seeking and who reject the truth and follow evil, there will be wrath and anger.'*
>
> (Romans 2:5-8)

Now read chapters 17 to 20.

f. The fall of Babylon and Satan

Notice the breathtaking picture of Christ's coming for judgment:

> *'I saw heaven standing open and there before me was a white horse, whose rider is called Faithful and True. With justice he judges and makes war. His eyes are like blazing fire, and on his head are many crowns. He has a name written on him that no-one knows but he himself. He is dressed in a robe dipped in blood, and his name is the Word of God. The armies of heaven were following him, riding on white horses and dressed in fine linen, white and clean. Out of his mouth comes a sharp sword with which to strike down the nations. "He will rule them with an iron sceptre" [Psalm 2:9]. He treads the winepress of the fury of the wrath of God Almighty. On his robe and on his thigh he has this name written: King of kings and Lord of lords.'*
>
> (19:11-16)

We see in this section that the things which the present world-system has to offer can never satisfy. Indeed, they are doomed to destruction:

> *'Do not love the world or anything in the world. If anyone love the world, the love of the Father is not in him. For everything in the world — the cravings of sinful man, the lust of his eyes and the boasting of what he has and does — comes not from the Father but from the world. The world and its desires pass away, but the man who does the will of God lives for ever.'*
>
> (1 John 2:15-17)

After the final overthrow of Satan we have yet another description of Christ's coming in judgment:

'The devil, who deceived them, was thrown into the lake of burning sulphur, where the beast and the false prophet had been thrown. They will be tormented day and night for ever and ever. Then I saw a great white throne and him who was seated on it. Earth and sky fled from his presence, and there was no place for them.'

(20:10-11)

Finally, read chapters 21 and 22.

g. Everything made new

In these concluding chapters we witness the consummation of this age, the ultimate victory of the Lamb and his church. At last, the present universe flees to make room for the new heaven and new earth, and the new Jerusalem:

'I saw a new heaven and a new earth, for the first heaven and the first earth had passed away, and there was no longer any sea. I saw the Holy City, the new Jerusalem, coming down out of heaven from God, prepared as a bride beautifully dressed for her husband.'

(21:1-2)

And what of the saints? Already, in the 'thousand years', they live and reign with Christ, the victor, on heavenly thrones. After the final judgment (20:11-15), these saints will reign for ever and ever (22:5) in the new heaven and new earth, with *everything* made new (21:3-5) and all opposition vanquished.

'The angels who did not keep their positions of authority but abandoned their own home — these he has kept in darkness, bound with everlasting chains for judgment on the great Day.'

(Jude 6)

'In all these things we are more than conquerors through him who loved us.'

(Romans 8:37)

'He made known to us the mystery of his will according to his good pleasure, which he purposed in Christ, to be put into effect when the times will have reached their fulfilment — to bring all things in heaven and on earth together under one head, even Christ.'

(Ephesians 1:9-10)

Study questions on Chapter 3: John's Approach

1. In what ways is Revelation:

   a. an unveiling?
   b. a prophecy?
   c. an epistle?

2. Examine the six assurances given to Christians under 'The purpose of the book' (section 2). How are these same assurances important to us today?

3. What is the relationship between the visible and invisible realms of struggle? How is the spiritual conflict between Satan and Jesus manifested here on earth in our lives?

4. Compare the different 'end of the age' accounts given in Revelation. How are they similar/different? How do they together give a full view of the end of the world?

5. Circle the word 'seven' each time it appears in the book of Revelation. How does the idea of seven as completeness or fulness correspond to the theme of Revelation?

6. In what ways have the major events of Revelation already happened? In what ways are they happening today? In what ways will they happen in the future?

True or False

1. Apocalypse means 'end times'.

2. The theme of Revelation is 'living the Christian life in the last days'.

3. The book's purpose is 'to comfort the churches in their struggle against the forces of evil'.

4. God has chosen to restrain himself from breaking in on man's world so as to keep man's free will intact.

5. As Christians, we live simultaneously in both this world and the world to come.

6. The book of Revelation can be divided into two struggles: one visible (the world against the church) and one invisible (the devil against Jesus).

7. The book of Revelation reveals a progression in depth or intensity of spiritual conflict.

8. The seven main sections in Revelation are complete in themselves and have little or no relationship between each other.

9. Each of the main sections spans the entire age from the first to the second coming of Christ, right to the end of the world as we know it.

10. The teachings of Revelation present information not revealed in any other part of the Bible.

11. The book of Revelation could be summed up by this Scripture verse: 'I have told you these things, so that in me you may have peace. In this world you will have trouble. But take heart! I have overcome the world' (John 16:33).

True or False

1.F 2.F 3.T 4.F 5.T 6.T 7.T 8.F 9.T 10.F 11.T

II

An Outline Analysis of Revelation

4

Christ and the Seven Churches

Outline analysis chapters 1 — 3

As we have seen, the book of Revelation consists of various sections, each of them spanning the entire church age from the first coming to the second coming of Christ, and beyond. These sections are like different transparencies laid one on top of another on an overhead projector to form one complete picture.

In this chapter we begin a more detailed outline analysis of the book, focusing first on Revelation 1 to 3. It is vital to bear in mind throughout that Revelation was written to seven real churches of John's generation:

> *'John, To the seven churches in the province of Asia'.*
>
> (1:4)

Yet there is a sense in which it is written to the church of *every* generation, for this book deals with the consummation of God's ultimate intention. This vision of the church doesn't relate exclusively to the circumstances of one particular period of history, but to events which are constantly repeated in the life of the church throughout the age.

The church is always in tribulation and surrounded by the darkness of this world. According to the New Testament, this isn't a world system that is getting better day by day, but one which is under judgment and whose condemnation is an accomplished fact. Jesus said:

> *'Now is the time for judgment on this world; now the prince of this world will be driven out. But I, when I am lifted up from the earth, will draw all men to myself.'*
>
> (John 12:31-32)

Now we begin our outline analysis with —

Christ and the Seven Churches

(chapters 1 — 3)

1. The central theme

The central theme of the first three chapters of Revelation is the glorified Christ in the midst of the seven golden lampstands. These seven lampstands represent the seven churches. The seven 'stars' represent the eldership of the various churches:

> *'The mystery of the seven stars that you saw in my right hand and of the seven golden lampstands is this: The seven stars are the angels of the seven churches, and the seven lampstands are the seven churches.'*
>
> (1:20)

As we have seen, the number seven occurs again and again in Revelation. It is everywhere symbolic of spiritual *completeness* or perfection:

> *'By the seventh day God had finished the work he had been doing; so on the seventh day he rested from all his work. And God blessed the seventh day and made it holy, because on it he rested from all the work of creating that he had done.'*
>
> (Genesis 2:2-3)

The first chapter introduces an important event which permeates the background of the rest of the book, namely, the coming of Christ in glory:

> *'Look, he is coming with the clouds, and every eye will see him, even those who pierced him; and all the peoples of the earth will mourn because of him. So shall it be! Amen.'*
>
> (1:7)

The whole book sheds light from above: the light of the coming Lord upon present circumstances and upon the things which will happen hereafter, in their development in history.

2. The glorified Christ

Christ, who walks in the midst of the seven golden lampstands in heaven, is also in the midst of his churches in the world. He is their light and life. Without him they are nothing and can do nothing. His various garments symbolise his ministry to the churches:

> *'I turned round to see the voice that was speaking to me. And when I turned I saw seven golden lampstands, and among the lampstands was someone "like a son of man", dressed in a robe reaching down to his feet and with a golden sash around his chest.'*
>
> (1:12-13)

He is in their midst as their merciful *high priest*, praying on their behalf and blessing them with all the blessings of salvation.

He is with them as their *mighty king*, ruling over them by his grace and his Spirit, protecting them in the midst of hateful enemies and leading them to victory and glory.

He also comes to the churches as their *righteous judge*. He commends whatever good is found in them. He rebukes them for their sins and weaknesses, calling them to repentance and threatening them with his wrath and judgments. It is because Christ is in the midst of his churches in the world as their judge that they must always seek to mend their ways.

He is also in their midst as their *prophet*, instructing them through his Spirit and Word and enabling them to know what must shortly come to pass. The sharp two-edged sword of his mouth is always active to separate soul (self) from spirit:

> *'The word of God is living and active. Sharper than any double-edged sword, it penetrates even to dividing soul and spirit, joints and marrow; it judges the thoughts and attitudes of the heart.'*
>
> (Hebrews 4:12)

3. Each church an illustration

Each individual church illustrates conditions in the church in every generation, circumstances which are constantly repeated in the life of Christ's church right through time to the end of the age. Each of the seven churches has its special lessons to teach us today:

a. Ephesus — the beginning of decline
b. Smyrna — strong in tribulation
c. Pergamum — growing lax in discipline
d. Thyatira — a mystical tendency
e. Sardis — about to die
f. Philadelphia — the promise of an open door
g. Laodicea — disgusting to the Lord

Each of the seven letters follows a general format consisting of:

☐ A commendation

☐ A condemnation

☐ A command

☐ A counsel

4. The seven churches

a. Ephesus — the beginning of decline

Ephesus was an important city, rich in trade and commerce. It was also rich in idolatry, frivolity and worldly-mindedness. It could be compared with one of our modern metropolitan cities with its wealth, amusement-seeking, vices and social evils. It is remarkable that, in such a city, the church had at first been so strong.

☐ Ephesus commendation: Hard work and perseverance

> *'I know your deeds, your hard work and your perseverance. I know that you cannot tolerate wicked men, that you have tested those who claim to be apostles but are not, and have found them false. You have persevered and have endured hardships for my name, and have not grown weary.'*
>
> (2:2-3)

This is a beautiful testimony, especially when seen in contrast with the serious rebuke which follows. It was a church full of action and good deeds. The people worked hard for God and his kingdom. There was sound teaching by competent teachers, exposing false apostles. Righteousness was important to them — they refused to tolerate wickedness. And they persevered in all sorts of hardships without giving up through tiredness.

☐ Ephesus condemnation: Forsaking of first love

Nevertheless, there was a certain defect in the inner life of the church, hidden perhaps from the naked eye but known to the Lord. A defect so serious that it would lead the church to utter ruin unless they were to repent:

> 'I hold this against you: You have forsaken your first love.'
>
> (2:4)

This is why we characterise the Ephesian church as in the 'beginning' of decline. In the abandoning of first love — for Christ and for each other — we can recognise the beginning of all apostasy in churches throughout the world in every century. Departure from the truth, laxity in church discipline, a tendency towards worldly-mindedness — these may be the first *symptoms* of spiritual decline, but they aren't the root.

How is it possible for a church to abandon its first love? By neglecting the necessity for personal faith and love in the Lord. Outwardly the church has grown, inwardly it has become weak. Worship and teaching have become automatic or professional; growth in numbers is thought to be more important than spiritual growth; instruction of the young isn't taken seriously; prestige becomes a priority.

The Lord speaks this warning to the church in the first stages of its spiritual decadence. There were still members who retained the love of the Lord in their hearts, and no doubt the fact that the Lord could speak so well of the church was in large measure due to their influence.

☐ Ephesus command: Remember and repent

> *'Remember the height from which you have fallen! Repent and do the things you did at first. If you do not repent, I will come to you and remove your lampstand from its place.'*
>
> (2:5)

The call to repentance is urgent. The Lord threatens the church with an end to their testimony if they do not comply: the loss of the lampstand means that the church would cease to be a manifestation of the body of Christ on earth.

Outwardly, as a mere human fellowship, it might continue to exist for some time, but it would no longer be representative of Christ. Like so many of the dead churches we see in the world today, it would be no more than a man-centred organisation, without the light of truth and the life of Christ.

☐ Ephesus counsel: Eat from the tree of life

> *'To him who overcomes, I will give the right to eat from the tree of life, which is in the paradise of God.'*
>
> (2:7)

The Lord closes this letter, not with the threat of judgment, but with an encouraging word of promise to those who overcome and remain faithful to the end in spite of opposition. Sadly, that opposition may come even from *within* the church. But the faithful will surely overcome. They will have the right to eat from the tree of life in the paradise of God.

b. Smyrna — strong in tribulation

☐ Smyrna commendation: You are rich

The best commendation is that there is *no condemnation* in this letter!

> *'I know your afflictions and your poverty — yet you are rich! I know the slander of those who say they are Jews and are not, but are a synagogue of Satan.'*
>
> (2:9)

The church in Smyrna is shown to be rich and strong, in spite of tribulation. This church is rich in the knowledge of the truth; rich in works and patience; rich in bearing the cross, revealing a strong spiritual life in the midst of persecution.

☐ Smyrna command: Do not be afraid

Because there is no condemnation, the command is an encouragement:

'Do not be afraid of what you are about to suffer. I tell you, the devil will put some of you in prison to test you, and you will suffer persecution for ten days.'

(2:10)

'Do not be afraid'! This is the positive message of the Lord to the church in tribulation. He not only cautions them in advance so that they may be fully prepared, but he also comforts and encourages them to face the future without fear.

In their own strength they would never be able to stand this persecution, but by the grace of God they will certainly endure, and, as a result, his name will be glorified:

'Be faithful, even to the point of death, and I will give you the crown of life.'

(2:10)

This is applicable to churches in every age. The devil may possess power to oppress the church, but her blessed comfort lies in the fact that the power of darkness is under the absolute control and sovereignty of him who walks among the seven golden lampstands.

☐ Smyrna counsel: Listen to the Spirit

'He who has an ear, let him hear what the Spirit says to the churches. He who overcomes will not be hurt at all by the second death.'

(2:11)

What does the Spirit say to us today? Be faithful until death. Don't seek the things of this world, for they soon pass away and behind them lurks the 'second death'. We live in serious times, serious because we hear of war and rumours of war as never before, yet still more serious because of the growing inclination to drift away from the truth and from the fulness of salvation that is available to us in Christ Jesus.

The overcomer might face death in persecution but will have life in eternity — no second death for him!

c. Pergamum — growing lax in discipline

'To the angel of the church in Pergamum write: These are the words of him who has the sharp, double-edged sword.'

(2:12)

The church in Pergamum occupies a dangerous position, for the text tells us that Pergamum is the place where Satan dwells — where his very throne is established.

This church has one characteristic which distinguishes it from the two previous churches: it tolerates evil men and is therefore the church which is growing lax in discipline.

☐ Pergamum commendation: Remaining true to Christ's name

Throughout this age Satan is the instigator of all opposition against the churches of Christ. This city is portrayed as a stronghold where the devil could have full and undisputed sway, were it not for this stronghold of Christ in the centre of a sinful city.

> *'I know where you live — where Satan has his throne. Yet you remain true to my name. You did not renounce your faith in me, even in the days of Antipas, my faithful witness, who was put to death in your city — where Satan lives.'*
>
> (2:13)

In principle, the position of the church in Pergamum is the same as that of today's church in relation to a world dominated by humanism and self-worship. Today, man sees himself as his own saviour, his own god.

Satan's dwelling-place is in many a school, college and university, where Christ is humanised and man is deified; where the worship of humanity is boldly preached; and where the blood of Christ is trampled underfoot. Paul writes of 'the man of lawlessness':

> *'He will oppose and will exalt himself over everything that is called God or is worshipped, so that he sets himself up in God's temple, proclaiming himself to be God.'*
>
> (2 Thessalonians 2:4)

Still worse, the devil has succeeded in ousting the true Saviour from many a Christian church. The true revelation of Christ is no longer proclaimed from many modern pulpits. The 'gospel' is often so distorted that Jesus can't be recognised!

☐ Pergamum condemnation: Lax in discipline

Though flourishing spiritually and faithful to the Lord, the church in Pergamum is defective in discipline — the discipline of its own members:

> *'I have a few things against you: You have people there who hold to the teaching of Balaam, who taught Balak to entice the Israelites to sin by eating food sacrificed to idols and by committing sexual immorality.'*
>
> (2:14)

Discipline is the Christ-ordained sentinel in the church. Without it the church is exposed to evil, to the seduction of false doctrine and to the degenerating influence of the world upon the life of its individual members.

☐ Pergamum command: Repent

> *'Repent therefore! Otherwise, I will soon come to you and will fight against them with the sword of my mouth.'*
>
> (2:16)

Conditions in Pergamum are not as precarious as those in Ephesus (the church which was losing its first love) and therefore the church isn't threatened with the removal of its lampstand.

Because the sole defect is a weakness in discipline, the Lord will come with the double-edged sword, his prophetic word, to separate spirit and soul, in order that the church may repent and excommunicate the impenitent evil-doers.

☐ Pergamum counsel: Aspire to the hidden manna and a new name

> *'He who has an ear, let him hear what the Spirit says to the churches. To him who overcomes, I will give some of the hidden manna. I will also give him a white stone with a new name written on it, known only to him who receives it.'*
>
> (2:17)

What does the Spirit say? Be diligent and do not remove the

sentinel of discipline. Don't allow evil men to remain in the midst of the church of Christ. Never allow them to camouflage the distinction between the church and the world. Then you will receive the hidden manna and a new (secret) name.

d. Thyatira — a mystical tendency

☐ Thyatira commendation: Love, faith, service, perseverance

> *'To the angel of the church in Thyatira write: These are the words of the Son of God, whose eyes are like blazing fire and whose feet are like burnished bronze. I know your deeds, your love and faith, your service and perseverance, and that you are now doing more than you did at first.'*
>
> (2:18-19)

Here we have a church apparently similar in many respects to the church at Pergamum. The difference in their shortcomings seems to be Thyatira's tendency towards mysticism.

☐ Thyatira condemnation: Mystical tendency

> *'I have this against you: You tolerate that woman Jezebel, who calls herself a prophetess. By her teaching she misleads my servants into sexual immorality and the eating of food sacrificed to idols.'*
>
> (2:20)

The woman propagating this heresy is named after, and thus likened to, one of the most despicable female characters of the Old Testament, Jezebel. She is being allowed to teach her contemptible doctrine regardless of the Bible's constant plea for sound doctrine:

> *'You must teach what is in accord with sound doctrine.'*
>
> (Titus 2:1)

This lovable church, strong in warm devotional life, had apparently forgotten to apply the objective standard of God's Word, allowing personal experience to be the criterion of truth.

This emphasis on personal experience led to a false mysticism. Satan employed a woman to appeal to the mystical tendency in the church, in order to seduce it from the truth.

> *'Adam was formed first, then Eve. And Adam was not the one deceived; it was the woman who was deceived and became a sinner.'*
>
> (1 Timothy 2:13-14)

☐ Thyatira command: Repent of your ways

The church should be on its guard against extremes: it must avoid the danger of cold intellectualism, but at the same time refuse to allow emotional experience to replace the revelation of the Word.

☐ Thyatira counsel: 'Hold on to what you have until I come' (2:25)

> *'To him who overcomes and does my will to the end, I will give authority over the nations — "He will rule them with an iron sceptre; he will dash them to pieces like pottery" — just as I have received authority from my Father. I will also give him the morning star. He who has an ear, let him hear what the Spirit says to the churches.'*
>
> (2:26-29)

What does the Spirit say? Don't drift away on emotional experience, ignoring the stated principles of the Word of God, for the Word is our only firm basis in the strong currents of human theory and false doctrine.

False doctrine may hide under a beautiful mask. In Thyatira it was a mask of super-piety. In our day it is often the mask of service to humanity. Service is good only if it is directed to God, not merely to man, and if it is based not on the vain theories of human philosophy but on the eternal principles of God's Word.

To the overcomers there is the promise of having authority — ruling the nations.

e. Sardis — about to die

☐ Sardis commendation: A few worthy ones

Sadly, there is no commendation for the church as a whole, only for a few of its members:

> *'You have a few people in Sardis who have not soiled their clothes. They will walk with me, dressed in white, for they are worthy.'*
>
> (3:4)

The world and the flesh dominated this church, though there were a few in Sardis who had not defiled their garments. The leaders of the church, in their Christian walk, couldn't be distinguished from the world. And those of the flock who did walk according to the precepts of the gospel were despised and considered narrow-minded.

☐ Sardis condemnation: You are dead

> *'To the angel of the church in Sardis write: These are the words of him who holds the seven spirits of God and the seven stars. I know your deeds; you have a reputation of being alive, but you are dead.'*
>
> (3:1)

There was no interest in the things of the kingdom of God, no searching of the Scriptures, no daily prayer, no confession of the name of Christ. Instead there was a seeking after the things of the flesh, a compromise with the world, a lusting after the luxuries for which Sardis was noted.

☐ Sardis command: Wake up and repent

> *'Wake up! Strengthen what remains and is about to die, for I have not found your deeds complete in the sight of my God. Remember, therefore, what you have received and heard; obey it, and repent.'*
>
> (3:2)

This church had fallen into a deep spiritual slumber; there was little activity in the church and none into the needy world outside it — little manifestation of spiritual life. The whole church was on the point of spiritual death.

The fact that the Lord praises the few faithful ones for not defiling their garments indicates that the other members had defiled theirs, living in open sin.

☐ Sardis counsel: Aim for the white garments and a place in the book of life

> *'He who overcomes will . . . be dressed in white. I will never blot out his name from the book of life, but will acknowledge his name before my Father and his angels. He who has an ear, let him hear what the Spirit says to the churches.'*
>
> (3:5-6)

The Spirit says, 'Be careful!' Many churches today have fallen asleep. There are numerous churches and ministers which, in spite of their reputation for being alive, are in fact dead. They have defiled their garments. We need to keep ours clean, remaining faithful and, by the grace of God, fighting the good fight to the end. Watch, therefore, that no-one takes your crown!

Overcomers will be dressed in white, with their names written in the book of life.

f. Philadelphia — the promise of an open door

Of all the seven churches, only two receive praise and consolation without any rebuke: Smyrna and Philadelphia. They are similar in their general description and characterisation by the Lord Jesus. Both are small and of little strength, both are enduring persecution and both have the same enemies: the 'natural' Jews of the day.

☐ Philadelphia commendation: You have kept my Word

There seems to be one difference: the church in Smyrna evidently spends all her spiritual strength in withstanding persecution, while the Philadelphia church still has opportunity to spread the gospel and gain converts, especially from among the Jews in the city:

> *'I know your deeds. See, I have placed before you an open door that no-one can shut. I know that you have little strength, yet you have kept my word and have not denied my name.'*
>
> (3:8)

This promise matches the desire of the church to add to their little flock by means of the preaching of the gospel. The church in Philadelphia is characterised by zeal for the Lord's cause and a determination to extend the kingdom of God.

This picture is of great significance for today's church. The Lord fulfils his strength in weakness. Today's church often forgets that it has little strength in itself. Let us remember that we cannot open and shut without the Lord. We are *his* church, to be used by him as his instrument.

☐ Philadelphia command: Hold on, I am coming

The Lord gives them a promise — 'I will . . . keep you from the hour of trial' (3:10) — and an encouragement:

> *'I am coming soon. Hold on to what you have, so that no-one will take your crown.'*
>
> (3:11)

☐ Philadelphia counsel: Aspire to be a pillar in God's temple

> *'Him who overcomes I will make a pillar in the temple of my God. Never again will he leave it. I will write on him the name of my God and the name of the city of my God, the new Jerusalem, which is coming down out of heaven from my God; and I will also write on him my new name. He who has an ear, let him hear what the Spirit says to the churches.'*
>
> (3:12-13)

What does the Spirit say? Being of little outward strength, in the task that they are called to perform and the tribulation to be suffered, this church must remember that they cannot rely on their own strength.

In the midst of suffering for Christ's sake, the vision of the mighty King of kings must always be before the church. His grace will keep us. With our eyes on him we may be sure of victory, which will be brought to completion at the coming of the Lord. Then we will be pillars in God's temple.

g. Laodicea — disgusting to the Lord

☐ Laodicea condemnation: You are lukewarm and poor

For this church there is no *commendation* at all — only blame!

> *'I know your deeds, that you are neither cold nor hot. I wish you were either one or the other! So, because you are lukewarm — neither hot nor cold — I am about to spit you out of my mouth.'*
>
> (3:15-16)

The general condition of the Laodicean church is 'neither hot nor cold'. Think of a drink — a hot drink can be pleasing, a cold one can be refreshing, but a lukewarm one is disgusting.

> *'You say, "I am rich; I have acquired wealth and do not need a thing." But you do not realise that you are wretched, pitiful, poor, blind and naked.'*
>
> (3:17)

The church's view of itself was exactly the opposite of the picture which Jesus drew: he said they were poor; they thought they were rich and in need of nothing. They were blind to the fact that they were the object of God's wrath and that, apart from his mercy and compassion, they would be lost. It was this self-indulgent attitude that made her so disgusting to the Lord.

☐ Laodicea command: Be earnest and repent

There is much self-satisfaction and self-righteousness in the church today which is alarmingly similar to the church of Laodicea. Today's church is sadly lacking in self-knowledge concerning sin and spiritual poverty.

Ministers of the gospel must carry a large part of the blame. Few of them preach repentance from sin and we rarely hear about man's depravity and guilt. The gospel of the cross, and of the righteousness of Christ received by faith alone, is disappearing from our pulpits.

The Christ of Galilee may be preached, but not the Christ of Calvary. The social Christ may be held up as our example while the Suffering Servant is often lost to our sight.

> *'Those whom I love I rebuke and discipline. So be earnest, and repent. Here I am! I stand at the door and knock. If anyone hears my voice and opens the door, I will come in and eat with him, and he with me.'*
>
> (3:19-20)

This is a word to churchgoers: Jesus is standing outside! Will the church listen to the rebuke? Of course, there will always be a faithful remnant in the church of Christ, and here the admonition to repent is addressed to individuals, rather than to the church as a whole.

If there is no repentance, the Lord will spit the church as a whole out of his mouth. It will cease to be a testimony to himself. But his own beloved, the elect of God, will not perish with the rest.

☐ Laodicea counsel: Aspire to be overcomers on the throne

> *'I counsel you to buy from me gold refined in fire, so that you can become rich; and white clothes to wear, so that you can cover your shameful nakedness; and salve to put on your eyes, so that you can see.'*
>
> (3:18)

Though there is no commendation at all for this church, there is still hope. If they open the door to Jesus they will see that they are poor, naked and blind, but also that Jesus gives them the opportunity to buy gold, white clothes and eye-salve from him.

Even to the members of this sadly defective church is given the prospect of being overcomers — and with what a promise!

> *'To him who overcomes, I will give the right to sit with me on my throne, just as I overcame and sat down with my Father on his throne.'*
>
> (3:21)

5. Each letter covers the entire church age

The seven letters give us a composite picture of the church in general at any period of her history: a mixture of light and darkness, qualities of good and evil, features both attractive and repulsive.

The *light* qualities are soundness in doctrine, faithfulness in administering discipline, energy in the work of the Lord, warmth and fulness of spiritual life, love, hope, confidence and patience in suffering for Christ's sake.

The *dark* features are coolness of spiritual life, lack of love, laxity in discipline, a tendency to false mysticism, lack of zeal in the work of the Lord and a combination of them all manifesting itself as a disgusting lukewarmness.

These first three chapters of Revelation, then, appear to span the entire age from Christ's first coming to save his people (1:5) to his second coming to judge all nations (1:7).

Study questions on Chapter 4: Christ and the Seven Churches

1. Examine the difficulties each of the seven churches had. Which ones, if any, do you see present in: a. your church? b. your own personal life? How can they be remedied?

2. What periods of tribulation have you endured? Consider the effects of enduring under trial (see Romans 5:1-5; James 1:2-4).

3. When and how should discipline be exercised in the church?

4. Which of the seven churches most represents your spiritual life? What action should you take as a result of realising this?

5. Make a list of the three qualities you would most like Jesus to commend you for. Earnestly pray and seek opportunities for these to be worked into your life.

True or False

1. The world is getting better day by day, even though things look bad outwardly.

2. The central theme of the first three chapters of Revelation is the glorified Christ in the midst of the seven golden lampstands.

3. Christ comes to his church as high priest, king, judge and prophet.

4. Each church mentioned in Revelation is an illustration of the conditions of one definite period of history.

5. Forsaking your love for the Lord is the final sign of spiritual decline.

6. The church at Smyrna had grown strong and was well able to withstand on its own the tribulation it faced.

7. Discipline is the Christ-ordained sentinel in the church.

8. A church which allows emotional experience to be the criterion of truth is better off than one which embraces cold doctrine and intellectualism.

9. The Lord fulfills his strength in weakness. Too often the church forgets that it has little strength in itself.

10. The Lord spoke to the Laodicean church about being cold in their outward zeal for him.

True or False

1.F 2.T 3.T 4.F 5.F 6.F 7.T 8.F 9.T 10.F

5

The Lamb, the Seals and the Trumpets

Outline analysis chapters 4 — 11

In this chapter we continue our outline analysis of the book, covering two sections:

- ☐ The Lamb and the Seven-Sealed Scroll (4 — 7)
- ☐ The Seven Trumpets (8 — 11)

Revelation 4 brings us into heaven and shows us the throne-room. It provides a brief vision of the greatness, majesty, power and kingly authority of God. We must remember that what is shown us from this chapter onwards is both contemporary and cyclical. We can see the scenes throughout history, developing and repeating themselves with a force that increases in intensity until Christ comes to establish his own eternal kingdom in perfect righteousness.

The Lamb and the Seven-Sealed Scroll

(chapters 4 — 7)

1. The throne-room of God (4:1-11)

In chapter 4 we are shown the vision of the throne-room of God — a representation of the new order. This order will be perfected with the second coming of our Lord in glory.

> *'I looked, and there before me was a door standing open in heaven. And the voice I had first heard speaking to me like a trumpet said, "Come up here, and I will show you what must take place after this." '*
>
> (4:1)

The difference between the vision in chapters 1 — 3 and this vision is the change of scene. The first vision was on earth and had a geographical and historical background, but now the scene has moved to heaven:

> *'At once I was in the Spirit, and there before me was a throne in heaven with someone sitting on it.'*
>
> (4:2)

John is called to heaven and presented with a view of earthly happenings from the perspective of him who sits upon the throne.

a. The throne

The word 'throne', symbolising power, occurs fourteen times in this chapter. This vision, which is closely related to the letters to the churches (chapters 1 — 3), shows what power is available for the church in its struggle. Persecuted Christians can feel safe only if they are sure of God's protecting care. This chapter makes us vividly conscious of the sovereignty of God, which is the comfort of the believer in every trial.

> *'The one who sat there had the appearance of jasper and carnelian. A rainbow, resembling an emerald, encircled the throne.'*
>
> (4:3)

b. The twenty-four elders

The throne, the focal point of the vision, is surrounded by twenty-four elders. These are to be taken as representatives of the entire church — the church redeemed and washed in the blood of the Lamb throughout the ages of history:

> *'The twenty-four elders fall down before him who sits on the throne, and worship him who lives for ever and ever. They lay their crowns before the throne.'*
>
> (4:10)

The elders sit on thrones themselves, indicating that they too possess a royal glory and dominion, one dependent upon the throne which they surround. They wear crowns of victory, for the church is pictured here from an ideal point of view: no longer as the church in tribulation but as it exists by God's decree, already victorious and therefore in heaven's eternal glory.

c. The four living creatures

> *'Also before the throne there was what looked like a sea of glass, clear as crystal. In the centre, around the throne, were four living creatures, and they were covered with eyes, in front and behind.'*
>
> (4:6)

The number of the creatures is significant: four is the number symbolic of creation and the earth (four seasons, four corners of the earth, etc.). These four creatures thus represent creation.

John must prophesy, as did Ezekiel in the Old Testament, the displacement of the old sinful order by that of the perfect order of the new creation. Then the kingdom of Christ will be complete and creation, with all its powers, will be 'delivered from the bondage of corruption into the glorious liberty of the children of God' (Romans 8:21 RAV).

> *'The creation waits in eager expectation for the sons of God to be revealed. For the creation was subjected to frustration, not by its own choice, but by the will of the one who subjected it, in hope that the creation itself will be liberated from its bondage to decay and brought into the glorious freedom of the children of God.'*
>
> (Romans 8:19-21)

2. The vision of the sealed scroll (5:1-14)

Jesus Christ is here shown receiving from God the power to do what no-one in all creation was worthy or able to do, namely, to bring to completion the glorious kingdom of God. Thus the chief thought of this chapter is that the Lamb — Jesus Christ — is found worthy to open the scroll.

a. The meaning of the scroll

> *'I saw in the right hand of him who sat on the throne a scroll with writing on both sides and sealed with seven seals.'*
>
> (5:1)

The number seven here implies that the thoughts of God in the scroll are complete and constitute an unalterable whole — nothing can be added to it or subtracted from it. The scroll is complete in itself (see also 22:18-19).

What is the significance of the scroll? The scroll symbolises the covenant of God, whose chief purpose is to see established the kingdom he planned from before the foundation of the universe. The breaking of the seals and the opening of the scroll signify the realisation of that kingdom.

b. Sealed with seven seals

The scroll is sealed with seven seals. The seal is a symbol of secrecy; it safeguards the contents from the eyes of those for whom they are not intended. The number seven, as we have seen, is connected with completeness — here in the context of the kingdom of God. When all these seals are loosed, the intentions of God will have been fulfilled and his kingdom will have been perfectly established in glory by the Lord Jesus Christ.

> *'I saw a mighty angel proclaiming in a loud voice, "Who is worthy to break the seals and open the scroll?" '*
>
> (5:2)

The profound silence which greets the angel's challenge represents humankind's vain efforts to work out their own own and the world's salvation, without dependence on the Lamb. At the heart of all trouble and confusion, all war and destruction, lie the guilt of sin and the corruption of people's nature. Human beings and society must undergo radical transformation: they must be regenerated, an operation possible only through the blood of the Lamb.

3. The slain Lamb (5:1-14)

The first picture we have of the Lord Jesus in chapter 5 is as a Lion-Lamb who has been slain and now rules from heaven:

> *'One of the elders said to me, "Do not weep! See, the Lion of the tribe of Judah, the Root of David, has triumphed. He is able to open the scroll and its seven seals." Then I saw a Lamb, looking as if it had been slain, standing in the centre of the throne, encircled by the four living creatures and the elders. He had seven horns and seven eyes, which are the seven spirits of God sent out into all the earth.'*
>
> (5:5-6)

Note that the Lamb stands in the midst of the throne, surrounded by the four living creatures and the twenty-four elders. He is the life and centre of them all, and his seven spirits are all-pervading.

All power in heaven and earth is surrendered into his hands; he now controls all history and is working out God's decree. He breaks seal after seal, as we shall see, and brings to pass all that must take place in the present age, with the intention of establishing the glorious kingdom of God.

When it is finally completed, and the power of the opposition has been broken, he will surrender his absolute power and subject himself and the perfectly completed kingdom to God the Father for ever and ever (1 Corinthians 15:26-28).

4. The seven seals opened (6:1 — 8:1)

The seven seals reveal the main aspects and currents of this present church age as they combine to carry out God's covenant. Every historical event possesses its own peculiar significance in the bringing of Christ's kingdom to its consummation. All the events of history, and all the factors which combine to create them, serve that one great purpose.

a. The first four seals (6:1-8)

The first four seals form a group distinguished from the other three by their symbolic figures: the horses and their riders. The appearing of each horse and rider is heralded by one of the four living creatures with the command, 'Come!'

> *'I watched as the Lamb opened the first of the seven seals. Then I heard one of the four living creatures say in a voice like thunder, "Come!"'*
>
> (6:1)

The fact that the horses and riders proceed from the scroll of God's covenant and are liberated to do their work at the bidding of the Lamb assures us that they will not run at random as blind powers or independent forces: each horse has a rider who directs it intelligently to a definite goal.

The identity of the riders is irrelevant. Horse and rider are one and reveal one idea: that all judgments are completely under the power of the Lamb 'looking as if it had been slain', to whom all power is given in heaven and on earth (Matthew 28:18).

b. The fifth seal (6:9-11)

> *'When he opened the fifth seal, I saw under the altar the souls of those who had been slain because of the word of God and the testimony they had maintained.'*
>
> (6:9)

The believers mentioned under this fifth seal have already fought the good fight and are evidently in heaven, waiting for their full adoption and the final glory. One of the chief purposes of this special seal is to show that the persecution of the believers, like other world events, is controlled by Jesus Christ and that the world's efforts have no effect unless the Lord allows it.

It is only when Jesus opens the seal that the martyrs cry for vengeance. The purpose of this seal is to assure us that the persecution of the believers is an element in the progress towards the completion of the kingdom of Christ.

c. The sixth seal (6:12-17)

While the fifth and sixth seals are closely related, there is a significant difference between them. Whereas the fifth seal deals with the suffering Christians in the world, the sixth seal refers to the effects of the shake-up of the world on the unrighteous:

> *'I watched as he opened the sixth seal. There was a great earthquake. The sun turned black like sackcloth made of goat hair, the whole moon turned blood red, and the stars in the sky fell to earth, as late figs drop from a fig-tree when shaken by a strong wind.'*
>
> (6:12-13)

Nothing can save the unrighteous and so they are overcome. They discover that the very basis of their imitation kingdom is doomed to destruction and that Christ's kingdom alone will prevail. They realise that their bitterest enemy, the King of heaven and earth, he whom they have pierced, is about to have the complete victory. In their folly and impotence they pray to the inanimate objects to protect them from God's wrath:

> *'They called to the mountains and the rocks, "Fall on us and hide us from the face of him who sits on the throne and from the wrath of the Lamb! For the great day of their wrath has come, and who can stand?" '*
>
> (6:16-17)

d. An interlude (7:1-17)

Before the opening of the seventh seal, there is an interlude in which the Lord comes to his people with a message of a different nature. In view of the terrible events of the six seals so far opened, the question asked by the unbelievers has undoubtedly arisen also in the minds of God's people, namely: 'Who can stand?'

The answer is provided in this first interlude. It contains two parts: the first in verses 1-8 and the second in verses 9-17.

It is important to understand this portion of Revelation in the symbolical sense consistent with the rest of the book. Israel should therefore be seen as the church of the new covenant (Galatians 6:16):

> *'It is not as though God's word had failed. For not all who are descended from Israel are Israel. Nor because they are his descendants are they all Abraham's children. On the contrary, "It is through Isaac that your offspring will be reckoned." In other words, it is not the natural children who are God's children, but it is the children of the promise who are regarded as Abraham's offspring.'*
>
> (Romans 9:6-8)

i. The 144,000 identified

Six seals have already been opened. They implied the suffering of God's people in the world. The seventh seal, still to be opened, will reveal even greater suffering and more terrible times. Hence the question: Shall we be able to stand? The answer is in the sealing of the 144,000 with the Spirit of our Lord Jesus:

> ' "*Do not harm the land or the sea or the trees until we put a seal on the foreheads of the servants of our God.*" *Then I heard the number of those who were sealed: 144,000 from all the tribes of Israel.*'
>
> (7:3-4)

The numbers ten and twelve (which combine to make up 144,000) are both significant. The number ten hints at God's covenant (ten commandments), while twelve represents God's people (twelve tribes, twelve apostles — the foundation of the church). Their interconnection and multiplication to 144,000, therefore, points to the complete number of God's elect people, reconciled by grace. The fact that they are from the twelve tribes of Israel hints at the distinctively Jewish character of the early church.

ii. The 144,000 sealed

What is implied in the 'sealing' of these 144,000? The seal symbol is common in both Old and New Testaments. Its most general idea seems to be that of security and safeguarding. The New Testament refers more than once to the sealing of the believers. For example:

> '*It is God who makes both us and you stand firm in Christ. He anointed us, set his seal of ownership on us, and put his Spirit in our hearts as a deposit, guaranteeing what is to come.*'
>
> (2 Corinthians 1:21-22)

> '*You . . . were included in Christ when you heard the word of truth, the gospel of your salvation. Having believed, you were marked in him with a seal, the promised Holy Spirit, who is a deposit guaranteeing our inheritance until the redemption of those who are God's possession — to the praise of his glory.*'
>
> (Ephesians 1:13-14)

Here the believers are sealed with the Holy Spirit. It is, therefore, a 'mark' placed on them to safeguard them against spiritual attack and make them invulnerable to spiritual destruction. It is a seal which will remain on them till the day of redemption. God's Spirit-filled people will be able to stand amid even the fiercest opposition.

iii. The great multitude

In verses 9-17 we see this same group of people (the 144,000) joined with the believers of all nations in eternal heavenly bliss. The vision reassures the believers that, from God's point of view, their salvation is secure, complete and perfect:

> *'I looked and there before me was a great multitude that no-one could count, from every nation, tribe, people and language, standing before the throne and in front of the Lamb.'*
>
> (7:9)

As the Lord's people, we are sealed for the day of redemption, completely safe, protected by the Lord. And we will never be lost!

e. The seventh seal (8:1)

The opening of the seventh seal caused a silence in heaven:

> *'When he opened the seventh seal, there was a silence in heaven for about half an hour.'*
>
> (8:1)

Directly after that we find the description of the seven trumpets. Therefore, it seems that the seven trumpets are a part of the seven-sealed scroll, a continuation of the preceding section.

The seven trumpets

(chapters 8 — 11)

> *'Another angel, who had a golden censer, came and stood at the altar. He was given much incense to offer, with the prayers of all the saints, on the golden altar before the throne. The smoke of the incense, together with the prayers of the saints, went up before God from the angel's hand.'*
>
> (8:3-4)

The incense here represents prayer. The saints, praying for the kingdom of God to come, receive a preliminary answer. These verses show us that our prayers aren't in vain, but that we can already see the answer to them here on earth. Only if we identify ourselves with the world do we fail to recognise the answer to those prayers and not see that God is bringing the kingdom to fulness according to his promise.

The practical lesson of this passage is that we should not be disturbed by the judgments of Christ which come upon the world. They are here now, and they must increase, for in no other way can the kingdom come. Sin and unrighteousness will develop, but they will be destroyed. The glory of Christ must be revealed and vindicated through his judgments upon the world:

> *'On that same night I will pass through Egypt and strike down every firstborn — both men and animals — and I will bring judgment on all the gods of Egypt. I am the Lord.'*
>
> (Exodus 12:12)

We must not be disturbed, therefore, but neither must we implore God to stop bringing in his kingdom by means of judgments. The prayers of the saints are certainly being answered, and the beginning of their fulfilment can be seen in these judgments (trumpets) of Christ upon earth. We should bring our prayers into harmony with the revealed will of God, praying, 'Hallowed be your name, your kingdom come, your will be done on earth as it is in heaven' (Matthew 6:9-10).

1. The first four trumpets (8:6-12)

The first four trumpets portray a level of judgment (one third of the universe affected) more severe than the seal-judgments (a quarter affected — 6:8). The Lamb controls the whole world and determines what must happen to complete his kingdom and ultimately destroy the power of all his enemies. In these 'natural' causes we see Christ, blowing the trumpets by means of the seven angels, determining developments on earth. The trumpets warn of the bowl-judgments to follow.

2. The fifth trumpet (8:13 — 9:11)

> *'Out of the smoke locusts came down upon the earth and were given power like that of scorpions of the earth. They were told not to harm the grass of the earth or any plant or tree, but only those people who did not have the seal of God on their foreheads. They were not given power to kill them, but only to torture them for five months.'*
>
> (9:3-5)

What is meant by this torment, and what is its nature? We must seek the answer in the description of the locusts themselves. They represent all that attracts the wicked world, everything that the world considers the source of bliss and salvation. They are the spirits who play on the passions of people. And they must incite men and women to go still further and give themselves up to all the pleasures of sin:

> *'They had tails and stings like scorpions, and in their tails they had power to torment people for five months.'*
>
> (9:10)

People will follow them fully, only to find they have a sting in the tail. They will be tortured by these demons on the rack of pessimism and despair:

> *'During those days men will seek death, but will not find it; they will long to die, but death will elude them.'*
>
> (9:6)

3. The sixth trumpet (9:13-21)

With regard to the sixth trumpet, it is important to notice the condition of the civilised world at the time. This trumpet will find its consummation in the period immediately preceding the bowl-judgments and the coming of the Lord. And what will be the condition of society at this period? Here we are told:

> *'The rest of mankind that were not killed by these plagues still did not repent of the work of their hands; they did not stop worshipping demons, and idols of gold, silver, bronze, stone and wood — idols that cannot see or hear or walk. Nor did they repent of their murders, their magic arts, their sexual immorality or their thefts.'*
>
> (9:20-21)

These last days were also described by Paul in his second letter to Timothy:

> *'Mark this: There will be terrible times in the last days. People will be lovers of themselves, lovers of money, boastful, proud, abusive, disobedient to their parents, ungrateful, unholy, without love, unforgiving, slanderous, without self-control, brutal, not lovers of the good, treacherous, rash, conceited, lovers of pleasure rather than lovers of God — having a form of godliness but denying its power. Have nothing to do with them.'*
>
> (2 Timothy 3:1-5)

All six trumpets symbolise the continuous effects of sin and evil. In answer to the cry of the martyrs to God, they portray how men and women for ever suffer from their disobedience to God. They also show how, in their rebellion and blindness, people will not recognise the results of their sin, and repent. Indeed, they grow more and more reckless and, as a result, call down still heavier judgments from God.

4. An interlude (10:1 — 11:14)

Before John describes the last trumpet of judgment, he places another interlude in the writing to emphasise the opportunities

God gives people to escape. Both interludes (between the sixth and seventh seals and the sixth and seventh trumpets) are designed to comfort the people of God.

> *'I saw another mighty angel coming down from heaven. He was robed in a cloud, with a rainbow above his head; his face was like the sun, and his legs were like fiery pillars. He was holding a little scroll, which lay open in his hand.'*
>
> (10:1-2)

The description of the angel shows his celestial dignity and glory (compare 5:2). God's glory is reflected in his messenger, as it once was in Moses (Exodus 34:29-35). The fact that the angel is seen 'coming down from heaven' indicates that he is God's messenger.

> *'He swore by him who lives for ever and ever . . . and said, "There will be no more delay! But in the days when the seventh angel is about to sound his trumpet, the mystery of God will be accomplished, just as he announced to his servants the prophets." '*
>
> (10:6-7. See also Matthew 24:48-50; Hebrews 10:37)

The visions of the first six trumpets have shown that the ungodly will not escape judicial retribution. But the six judgments don't bring repentance. Therefore, there can be no more delay in the fulfilment of the seventh trumpet (compare 6:10).

a. The little scroll (10:8-11)

> *'The voice that I had heard from heaven spoke to me once more: "Go, take the scroll that lies open in the hand of the angel who is standing on the sea and on the land." '*
>
> (10:8)

So far, John has merely recorded what he has heard and seen. But now he becomes an actor in the drama, and his part is to eat the little scroll.

This symbolic language is based on Ezekiel 2:9 — 3:3. The taking of the little scroll represents the acceptance by the prophet of the commission to which he was called. As the scroll in chapter

5 represents the covenant of God made effective by Christ, so the little scroll represents the part which is made effective through the witness of the church.

> *'I took the little scroll from the angel's hand and ate it. It tasted as sweet as honey in my mouth, but when I had eaten it, my stomach turned sour.'*
>
> (10:10)

John's commission was much to his liking, and he became personally involved in presenting it to the people. He soon found, however, that the sweet message became sour after he had eaten it.

The sweet mercies and bitter judgments of God are both a part of the one message. It is a double-edged sword (1:16), a message of the uncompromising sovereignty of God in Jesus Christ. To be admitted to the knowledge of the purpose of God in redemption is sweet (Jeremiah 15:16), but it is sour to carry to men a message of judgment.

b. The measuring of the temple (11:1-2)

The first part of chapter 11 continues the interlude between the sixth and seventh trumpets. It divides into two sections, the first describing the measuring of the temple (11:1-2) and the second the appearance and murder of two witnesses (11:3-14).

These two subsections show that nothing can violate the dwelling-place of God or destroy his witnesses until their testimony is complete. John uses these two events, employing biblical persons, objects and incidents, to convey spiritual truths applicable to all times.

> *'I was given a reed like a measuring rod and was told, "Go and measure the temple of God and the altar, and count the worshippers there. But exclude the outer court; do not measure it, because it has been given to the Gentiles. They will trample on the holy city for 42 months." '*
>
> (11:1-2)

The temple is a symbol of the church, called by Paul 'God's temple' (1 Corinthians 3:16), 'a holy temple' (Ephesians 2:21), 'the temple of the living God' (2 Corinthians 6:16) and 'a dwelling in which God lives by his Spirit' (Ephesians 2:21-22).

The basis of the vision is in Ezekiel 40 — 43 and Zechariah 2:1-5. It is like the sealing of the faithful in Revelation 7:1-8. The temple, altar and worshippers — everything necessary to worship — are measured. This measuring is continually going on. When everything else falls into the hands of the enemy, these are spared.

It means that the true church will be protected and preserved intact during persecution and the judgments of God. The Lord will protect and preserve his people in their trials and troubles.

c. The 42 months (1260 days or 3½ years)

These numbers symbolise persecution, limitation and incompleteness, the enigmatic three and a half being half the perfect number seven. The period is indefinite, but it will come to an end.

In Revelation, all these terms refer to the same period of time. The duration of prophesying is to correspond with the duration of the trampling under foot. John is told that the Gentiles — the unregenerate, the unbelievers — were to 'trample on' the court outside for an indefinite period.

This period covers the entire duration of the church's history on earth. John expresses his confidence that, throughout its history, the believing community will be supernaturally protected. In this march of progress, the church itself will suffer through unfaithfulness and worldliness, but the true church will be kept safe.

d. The power and authority of the two witnesses (11:3-14)

> *'I will give power to my two witnesses, and they will prophesy for 1260 days, clothed in sackcloth.'*
>
> (11:3)

The position of the true church isn't one of idle security. Christ must be proclaimed, and the task of the church is to preach the gospel even in the face of persecution. The 'two witnesses' are patterned after the biblical pictures of Moses (the Law) and Elijah (the Prophets), because of the conspicuous witness they had and the hardships they suffered, as well as their persecution and vindication.

The number and variety of interpretations given to the two witnesses are bewildering. In the light of John's use of the Old Testament, however, it seems that these two competent and confirmatory witnesses symbolise the true church (John 15:27; Acts 1:8). They represent the missionary activity of the whole church, which is called to bear its testimony during the 1260 days.

The two witnesses are to prophesy God's message of salvation and judgment. They will prophesy in the midst of grief, that is, while being trampled over by the world (Matthew 5:4). In heaven the witnesses wear white robes, but on earth they wear sackcloth.

e. Temporary defeat, ultimate triumph

> *'When they have finished their testimony, the beast that comes up from the Abyss will attack them, and overpower and kill them.'*
>
> (11:7)

The sufferings of the two witnesses follow the pattern of Jesus' sufferings. When he had finished his work, the power of evil seemed to prevail (John 17:4; 19:30). Like Jesus, the two witnesses are secure, seemingly indestructible and invincible, until their time of bearing full witness for God is accomplished (Acts 20:27).

The purpose of this vision is to show that the church in its witness for God will experience opposition from the power of Satan. The Beast made war against Christ and for a time seemed to have killed him. John's words 'cover in effect all the martyrdoms and massacres of history in which brute force has seemed to triumph over truth and righteousness'.[1]

---

1. H.B. Swete, *The Apocalypse of St John*, Macmillan, 1911.

'They heard a loud voice from heaven saying to them, "Come up here." And they went up to heaven in a cloud, while their enemies looked on.'

(11:12)

In describing the fate of the church, John seems to have in mind the life of Christ. Jesus' witness, the opposition he encountered, his death for a brief time at the completion of his work, his resurrection and ascension, and his triumph over the devil, are all here reproduced. John is saying that the same God who transformed Christ's death into life can transform the church's apparent defeat into victory.

'The second woe has passed; the third woe is coming soon.'

(11:14)

A voice now announces that, since two of the woes have passed, the third one is coming soon. The third woe is the final trumpet which ushers in the completion of the mystery of God. It pictures the rule of the Redeemer in triumph and implies the overthrow and passing away of all that opposes the Messiah's reign.

5. The seventh trumpet (11:15-19)

'The seventh angel sounded his trumpet, and there were loud voices in heaven, which said: "The kingdom of the world has become the kingdom of our Lord and of his Christ, and he will reign for ever and ever." '

(11:15)

The opening of the seventh *seal* was followed by 'silence in heaven' (8:1). The sounding of the seventh *trumpet* is accompanied by 'loud voices in heaven'. However, there is silence as to the fate of the wicked, with whom the trumpet visions have so far been chiefly concerned. Their doom is simply shown as consummated.

Rather, when the seventh trumpet sounds, instead of judgment falling, there is heard a chorus of heavenly voices praising God. The unidentified voices proclaim the replacement of the kingdom of the world by that of our Lord. John is reaffirming the great eternal reign of God in Christ, the rule of God in the lives of men and women.

The blowing of this seventh and last trumpet brings us once more to the consummation of all things. These visions, evoked by the cry for the vindication of righteousness in 6:10, have shown both the need for patience and endurance on the part of Christians, and also the punishments meted out to the wicked. This is the final triumph of the faithful. The entire scene represents an accomplished victory.

With the end of Revelation 11 we have obviously come to the end of another section of the book. The chapters that follow look at the same truths, but from a different viewpoint.

Study questions on Chapter 5: The Lamb, the Seals and the Trumpets

1. In Revelation 5 it is Jesus alone who is able to open the scroll; every other being falls short. Consider how our individual efforts to achieve God's purposes fall short of what Jesus alone can do through his body the church.

2. Think about situations in which you have cried out to the Lord to bring judgment on evil around you. How did he answer? How *will* he answer?

3. The sinful attractions which lure men and women only end up destroying them. How can we explain true fulfilment in Jesus to the people around us who are used to being disappointed and unsatisfied?

4. Discuss how God's Word is often sweet to the taste but difficult to digest.

5. Study the concept of being 'sealed' with the Spirit and meditate on scriptures which refer to it, such as Ephesians 1:13; 4.30; 2 Corinthians 1:21-22; 2 Timothy 2:19. How does this give you security?

6. In what ways have you seen God bring triumph out of apparent defeat? In which areas of your life do you need to believe God for this kind of victory?

7. Jesus' life — his witness, suffering, death, resurrection, ascension and glorification — parallel the destiny of the church. Find specific verses and examples in the New Testament which portray these parallels between the Lord and his church.

True or False

1. The visions in Revelation 4 — 7 give a heavenly viewpoint of earthly happenings.

2. The scroll which the Lamb opens is symbolic of God's decree to establish his kingdom.

3. Jesus is seen primarily as the Prince of Peace in chapters 4 — 7.

4. The identity of the four horses and riders in chapter 6 has a special significance which is revealed in the Old Testament.

5. The martyrdom of the believers is an element in the progress towards the completion of the kingdom of God.

6. Exactly 144,000 Christians will be raptured before the great tribulation.

7. The number 144,000 represents the complete number of God's chosen people on the earth in any period of this church age.

8. God brings judgment on the world in response to the prayers of his people who cry out for his kingdom to come.

9. The locusts of the fifth trumpet represent a terrible pestilence that will befall the nations of the earth.

10. John is asked to measure the temple which will be rebuilt in modern Jerusalem.

11. The time period 3½ years (1260 days, 42 months) represents an indefinite but limited amount of time.

True or False

1.T 2.T 3.F 4.F 5.T 6.F 7.T 8.T 9.F 10.F 11.T

6

The Battle and the Bowls

Outline analysis chapters 12 — 16

A further two sections are covered in this chapter:

☐ The Battle (12 — 14)

☐ The Seven Bowls of Wrath (15 — 16)

The Battle

(chapters 12 — 14)

In the previous sections, John has proclaimed God's sovereignty over the world in Jesus Christ. Now, taking a different viewpoint and using a different kind of picture, he portrays the manner in which this rule of God has been extended and how its extension precipitates the inevitable conflict with the powers of darkness.

Revelation gives no chronological disclosure of the conflict between good and evil. John proceeds instead by the use of interlocking spirals of material, dealing in much repetition and emphasising his main points over and over again.

Up to now, each of the series of visions has come to the same general conclusion: toil and trouble end in rest, and conflict ends in victory. The development from Revelation 12 to the end of the book is the account of the conflict between the sovereignty of God in Jesus Christ and the pretended sovereignty of Satan expressed through world power.

1. The war between the Lamb and the red dragon (12:1-6)

'Another sign appeared in heaven: an enormous red dragon with seven heads and ten horns and seven crowns on his head.'

(12:3)

The visions which now follow are different in character from the earlier ones in that the supernatural conflict is now described as between the powers of good and evil, heaven and hell, the Lamb and the red dragon, rather than between the individual Christian and his oppressors. But this spiritual strife with the forces of evil is still carried on through the church. In chapter 12, John uses various parallels to the experiences of Israel escaping from Egypt.

'His tail swept a third of the stars out of the sky and flung them to the earth. The dragon stood in front of the woman who was about to give birth, so that he might devour her child the moment it was born.'

(12:4)

John's object in the first part of this verse is to emphasise the dragon's size and strength. The dragon's primary interest is in devouring the child — the pre-existent Messiah — when he is born. The people of God are confronted by the epitome of evil at a crucial point in humankind's redemption: the incarnation of Christ.

'She gave birth to a son, a male child, who will rule all the nations with an iron sceptre. And her child was snatched up to God and to his throne.'

(12:5)

In this verse John tells the whole story of the incarnation and its fruits in language that is strong and symbolic. This vision sums up the entire earthly ministry of Jesus, his crucifixion, resurrection and ascension, because his purpose is to show that the dragon's power is futile.

Satan desires to devour the child because he regards the nations as his legitimate prey. But he was unable to destroy Christ while he was on earth. This symbolism stresses the truth that, in the incarnation, God has decisively defeated the devil. Jesus' cross was the battlefield where God's power met and overcame the demonic powers and triumphed over them openly (Colossians 2:15). At the incarnation, which was completed with the ascension, spiritual evil was completely defeated and dethroned.

2. The effects of the incarnation (12:7-12)

> *'There was war in heaven. Michael and his angels fought against the dragon, and the dragon and his angels fought back. But he was not strong enough, and they lost their place in heaven.'*
>
> (12:7-8)

The dragon and his army are routed and expelled from their former celestial place. This casting down of Satan by no means brings about his destruction. His appearance on the earthly scene is the signal for the continuation of the struggle on earth. He finds there a new stage on which to continue the conflict against God and all good.

Woe comes upon the earth because it is the battlefield, and the wrath of the devil is multiplied because he knows he has only a short time. God's mighty act in the resurrection of the Messiah is the great and final challenge to the dominion of Satan.

> *'Rejoice, you heavens and you who dwell in them! But woe to the earth and the sea, because the devil has gone down to you! He is filled with fury, because he knows that his time is short.'*
>
> (12:12)

Christ casts Satan from his throne for the benefit of those who faithfully trust and follow him. Satan can no longer accuse the brethren before God (12:10; Romans 8:1-2). Christ's birth and rapture meant the downfall of Satan, and every Christian victory confirms it. But even though he is defeated, Satan still has power to do considerable harm. His power, far from being annihilated by defeat, is actually stimulated by it.

In this symbolism, John shows the persistent hostility between Satan and the people of God. He is still permitted to inflict great sufferings on the servants of Christ, but these activities — like the ferocious roars of a dying lion — are the final convulsions of a conquered foe.

3. The dragon persecutes the woman's offspring (12:13-17)

> *'The dragon was enraged at the woman and went off to make war against the rest of her offspring — those who obey God's commandments and hold to the testimony of Jesus.'*
>
> (12:17)

The woman here seems to represent the church, while the war refers to persecutions against all individuals in the church who 'obey God's commandments and hold to the testimony of Jesus'.

The methods by which the devil endeavours to 'make war' are related in the following chapters. For this warfare, the dragon takes up his position at the side of the sea to summon and direct his subordinates (13:1). These helpers symbolise the resources of evil which are brought to bear upon Christians. They are Satan's agents on earth, commissioned to carry on his warfare against the church.

4. The beast out of the sea (13:1-10)

> *'The dragon stood on the shore of the sea. And I saw a beast coming out of the sea. He had ten horns and seven heads, with ten crowns on his horns, and on each head a blasphemous name.'*
>
> (13:1)

The word 'beast' denotes a fierce, untamed animal of the lower order. It implies the predominance of the bestial nature. The background of this symbol is Daniel 7:2-7. The sea from which the beast comes represents the confused, unstable, disorderly and rebellious multitudes of the nations, from which arise the enemies of the church. In the Old Testament, the sea is often used to describe a restless nation of people (see, for example, Jeremiah 49:23).

John doesn't identify this beast out of the sea but it seems to represent world power, the aggregation of forces opposed to God.

It is a term for all who are in the kingdom of darkness. It is human society estranged from God and organised in hostility against his purpose and will. It is also the embodiment of a sad and perilous order of life belonging to the present evil age. This order has in principle been brought to an end by the coming of Christ and is now doomed and in the process of passing away (1 John 2:17). It is human society under the domination of the evil one (1 John 5:19).

This same world power had previously expressed itself against God through Egypt, Assyria, Babylon, Persia, Greece, Syria and others.

> *'One of the heads of the beast seemed to have had a fatal wound, but the fatal wound had been healed. The whole world was astonished and followed the beast.'*
>
> (13:3)

The statement that the beast's 'fatal wound had been healed' is a parody of the death and resurrection of Christ (1:18; 5:6). When Christ was victorious over death, he sounded the death-knell for world power. However, the death-stroke is apparently healed, for world power continues to exist in spite of its fatal wound. If its dominion is overthrown, contrary to all expectations it rises again. Given a death-blow, it lives on under new forms and new names, seeming as strong as or even stronger than ever in its attacks upon the church. But these attacks are signs, not of continuing life, but of approaching death (17:11).

John says that 'the whole world was astonished and followed the beast'. World power is always able to command the homage of that worldly spirit to which it makes its appeal. Worldly power is not only persuasive and threatening; it is also at times very attractive.

> *'If anyone is to go into captivity, into captivity he will go. If anyone is to be killed with the sword, with the sword he will be killed. This calls for patient endurance and faithfulness on the part of the saints.'*
>
> (13:10)

This verse contains a prediction and a warning. The faithful believers can expect persecution and suffering, but they are not to defend themselves by the use of the sword.

The background seems to be Jeremiah 15:2 and 43:11. John affirms the principle upon which God's government of the world operates: sin must bring its reward of suffering and ultimate frustration. Christian insight into history consists of holding on to this clue. All power belongs to God and he is still in control, even when evil appears all-powerful.

5. The beast out of the earth (13:11-18)

> *'I saw another beast, coming out of the earth. He had two horns like a lamb, but he spoke like a dragon.'*
>
> (13:11)

The second beast differs from the first, to which he is auxiliary and subsidiary. He arises out of the earth, that is, out of settled human society. As the first beast symbolised world power, the second signifies the more subtle yet even deadlier power of false religion.

False religion is the personification of godless authority and the prostrating of man's instinctive religiousness and natural tendency to worship:

☐ It has no foundation in truth or reality and is one way men and women try to escape their restless consciences

☐ It places undue reliance upon externals and blends avarice and superstition

☐ It is supported by diabolical supernaturalism

☐ It has an abundance of rites of worship, but is averse to inward holiness and the entire submission of life to God

☐ It gives license to the sensual nature of men and women

☐ It proclaims an accommodation theology and separates religion from morality

☐ It seeks earthly advantage

False religion is one of the most inhuman forces in the world.

It encourages the wicked in their evil ways. It is hostile to true religion and seeks to overthrow the foundations of righteousness. It strives to arrest the process of God's reign and endeavours to make the worst things appear the best (Isaiah 5:20). It teaches that unrighteous lives can be compensated for by formal acts of religion.

> *'He exercised all the authority of the first beast on his behalf, and made the earth and its inhabitants worship the first beast, whose fatal wound had been healed.'*
>
> (13:12)

The second beast simulates miracles by satanic magic in order to induce people to worship the first beast. This 'false prophet' is the instrument of the revelation of satanic authority as the Holy Spirit is the mediator of God's revelation. All his actions suggest religious activities. The symbolism stands for any religious system which allies itself with world powers hostile to Christ and his church. It is that system which persuades humanity to worship evil under the guise of good.

This beast's 'two horns like a lamb' make him a parody of true religion. The church worships the Lamb, and so the symbol of false religion is a beast with two horns like a lamb. He appears gentle but speaks deceitfully as the dragon. This beast is also called the 'false prophet' (16:13; 20:10).

6. The mark of the beast (13:16-18)

> *'He also forced everyone, small and great, rich and poor, free and slave, to receive a mark on his right hand or on his forehead, so that no-one could buy or sell unless he had the mark, which is the name of the beast or the number of his name.'*
>
> (13:16-17)

The mark of the beast is a parody of the mark of God on his faithful ones (7:3), because everyone bears some mark to indicate his loyalty. In symbolic language, John says that, just as worshipping Christians are being transformed into Christ's likeness (2 Corinthians 3:18), the worship of world power transforms a person into the world's likeness.

The 'mark' is imprinted on a person's forehead or right hand in imitation of Israel and of God's commandments (Deuteronomy 6:6-8). The mark cannot be hidden, for a person increasingly reflects the image of his master. Worshippers are forced to show their loyalty to the beast in public ways, and if they refuse they are publicly ostracised. No-one who refuses the dominion of world power may enjoy its privileges.

> *'This calls for wisdom. If anyone has insight, let him calculate the number of the beast, for it is man's number. His number is 666.'*
>
> (13:18)

In accordance with John's symbolic method, it seems best to interpret this mysterious number, 666, as symbolic of incompleteness, falling short of seven, which was regarded as the number of perfection.

The number 666 expresses all that is possible for human wisdom and power to achieve when directed by an evil spirit. It indicates a state of marvellous earthly 'perfection', when the beast-power has reached its highest development. False religion always tries to persuade men and women to accept world power as a substitute for God, or at least as not antagonistic to him.

7. The Lamb and his followers (14:1-20)

a. Comfort in the certainty of victory (14:1-5)

> *'I looked, and there before me was the Lamb, standing on Mount Zion, and with him 144,000 who had his name and his Father's name written on their foreheads.'*
>
> (14:1)

This scene pictures the security and peace that belong to the people of God, the redeemed church (Isaiah 28:16; 51:11; Hebrews 12:22). The symbolic 144,000 is the same group as described in 5:9-10 and 7:1-8, and stands in contrast to those who worship the beast (13:12). It is the church's symbol of twelve reproduced and multiplied. It represents the whole church, the redeemed from the earth (14:3), in its ideal completeness and blessedness.

John sees all the faithful Christians standing in the presence of Christ with the name of God inscribed on their foreheads, in contrast to those who carry the mark of the beast (13:16). This seal, the mark of messianic salvation, has its root in the historical first coming of Jesus. The seal is a sign that the faithful Christians are for ever Christ's and thus are always under watchful care. These are the ones who have made the break with world power and walk with Christ in perfect security, whatever tribulation or persecution may come.

b. The triumph of the gospel (14:6-7)

> *'I saw another angel flying in mid-air, and he had the eternal gospel to proclaim to those who live on the earth — to every nation, tribe, language and people.'*
>
> (14:6)

In this symbolic vision, John saw 'another angel'. The word 'another' is a link to the former visions. The angel is 'flying in mid-air' and could therefore be seen and heard by the whole inhabited world. His message is intended for worldwide proclamation. The angel proclaims from heaven the universal 'eternal gospel' of God's victory. Its proclamation issues in a choice of either salvation or judgment.

c. The fall of Babylon is announced (14:8)

> *'A second angel followed and said, "Fallen! Fallen is Babylon the Great, which made all the nations drink the maddening wine of her adulteries." '*
>
> (14:8)

At the beginning of this chapter, John portrayed the blessedness of those who worship the Lamb; now he shows, with terrible imagery, the punishment of those who worship the beast. The second angel proclaims the fact that the great city of Babylon is fallen (compare 1 Peter 5:13). In the sight of God, Babylon has already fallen. Its death-blow has been dealt by the life, death and resurrection of Christ. It falls because this 'eternal gospel' has undermined world power. This fall is described at greater length in later visions (chapters 17 — 18).

d. The doom of the beast-worshippers (14:9-12)

'A third angel followed them and said in a loud voice: "If anyone worships the beast and his image and receives his mark on his forehead or on the hand, he, too, will drink of the wine of God's fury, which has been poured full strength into the cup of his wrath. He will be tormented with burning sulphur in the presence of the holy angels and of the Lamb." '

(14:9-10)

The third angel warns all the people not to identify themselves with world power and describes the retribution upon those who do so. No-one who worships the beast and his image can escape from bearing the mark of the beast. It is a law of life that the object of a man's devotion transforms him into its character. Therefore no-one can escape from bearing either 'the mark of the beast' or the mark of the name of Christ and the name of the Father (14:1).

The penalties for bearing the beast's mark are great and clear. Those with his mark share in his punishment. The imagery in which these penalties are described is almost wholly derived from the Old Testament (Jeremiah 25:15; Isaiah 51:17).

e. The harvesting of the saints (14:14-16)

'Another angel came out of the temple and called in a loud voice to him who was sitting on the cloud, "Take your sickle and reap, because the time to reap has come, for the harvest of the earth is ripe." '

(14:15)

The figure of the harvest is taken from Joel 3:12-13. In this figure, Joel pictured the deliverance of Judah and the judging of the nations. John uses this figure in a similar way.

The symbols clearly reflect Jesus' parable of the wheat and the tares (Matthew 13:24-30). The reaping represents the all-inclusive act of gathering the whole of humankind before God's judgment seat (Romans 14:10-12). The harvest symbolises the gathering of the redeemed, while the vintage symbolises the judgment of the unredeemed. In these verses the assurance of victory is demonstrated in the harvesting of God's elect.

f. The judgment of the church's enemies (14:17-20)

> *'The angel swung his sickle on the earth, gathered its grapes and threw them into the great winepress of God's wrath. They were trampled in the winepress outside the city, and blood flowed out of the press, rising as high as the horses' bridles for a distance of 1600 stadia.'*
>
> (14:19-20)

John mixes the metaphors of winepress and battlefield, the combination making the picture more terrible. In this dual symbolic representation, John portrays an appalling scene of judgment on the enemies of God. All evil is punished.

The 1600 stadia symbolise the whole world. The entire world, of which Satan is the prince, is judged, condemned and punished. The whole dreadful picture is intended to convey the awesome nature of the judgment and the completeness with which the powers of evil are overthrown. These forces of evil have seemingly achieved universal sway, but their overthrow is certain.

With the conclusion of this section, we are again brought to the end of the world and the final judgment.

The Seven Bowls of Wrath

(chapters 15 — 16)

In this section John sets forth in more detail the divine judgments upon the church's enemies: the dragon, the beast out of the sea and the false prophet. The 'bowl' symbol seems to be taken from the shallow bowls which were placed on the golden altar of Judaism and in which incense was burned (Exodus 30:1-10).

The vision of the bowls stresses the note of triumph. Each bowl contributes its part to the song of triumph of the redeemed. The writer uses much of the Exodus typology. Now we have a new 'Moses' (Christ) and a new 'Exodus' (of God's redeemed people from slavery to sin).

The fact that both the seals and the trumpets deal with the same theme (the victory of Christ and his church over evil) shows again that the various sections of Revelation run parallel, each giving a different aspect of the same temporal judgments during this church age. With each parallel the intensity increases.

In the vision of the bowls we have a recapitulation of what has already been given in the seal and trumpet visions. But it is more than plain repetition. The earlier ideas are now strengthened. The severity of the bowls-judgment is evident. Under the seals vision, a quarter of all is afflicted, and under the trumpets vision, a third. But there is no indication that *any* are exempt from the judgments of the bowls vision.

1. The seven last plagues (15:1)

> *'I saw in heaven another great and marvellous sign: seven angels with the seven last plagues — last, because with them God's wrath is completed.'*
>
> (15:1)

These bowl-plagues symbolise the ultimate expression of God's wrath against evil. His wrath is the consequence of the breaking of his laws, for sin and suffering are linked. God gives men and women time to repent; he is longsuffering and warns often, but the last time finally comes. He uses both natural and supernatural forces to bring judgment upon the disobedient.

2. Praise for God's just judgments (15:2-8)

> *'I saw what looked like a sea of glass mixed with fire and, standing beside the sea, those who had been victorious over the beast and his image and over the number of his name. They held harps given them by God.'*
>
> (15:2)

John sees those who have come victoriously out of the conflict with the enemies of the church (7:1-8; 14:1-5). The victory has been achieved over the enemies described in chapter 13. They stand in the very presence of God, where they are beyond the power of the dragon and his agents, having been faithful in their struggle against them.

The unusual combination of sea and fire seems to represent God's holiness and justice or purity and judgment (8:5). The whole scene is a preparation for what is to come in the outpouring of the bowls.

> *'Out of the temple came the seven angels with the seven plagues. They were dressed in clean, shining linen and wore golden sashes round their chests.'*
>
> (15:6)

It is out of the immediate presence of God that the angels come to serve as God's agents in fulfilling his covenant promise to bless his people and judge their enemies (Psalm 10:16-18; Isaiah 2:4; 54:5).

> *'One of the four living creatures gave to the seven angels seven golden bowls filled with the wrath of God, who lives for ever and ever.'*
>
> (15:7)

The 'four living creatures', representing the created world and all life on earth, are appropriately chosen as the agents for conveying to the seven angels the plagues of the seven bowls. These 'seven golden bowls', indicating completeness, are filled with God's wrath, just as the elders' bowls were filled with the prayers of the believers (5:8).

The laws and forces of nature, then, fill the bowls of wrath and place them in the hands of angels. The plagues within them are the penalties for breaking divine laws.

3. The first four bowls (16:1-9)

> *'I heard a loud voice from the temple saying to the seven angels, "Go, pour out the seven bowls of God's wrath on the earth." '*
>
> (6:1)

Revelation 16 relates the pouring out of the contents of the seven bowls. As each bowl of God's wrath is emptied, certain actions occur. Notice that the results of these actions bear a close resemblance to the opening of the seven seals and the sounding of the seven trumpets. This is John's method of emphasising the judgments by recapitulation. The major difference is that in the previous visions the punishments for sin were partial, and there was hope for repentance. In the bowls vision, the wrath of God is poured out on the whole heedless, ungodly world. The purpose is to enlist the natural order in the service of divine retribution.

> *'They were seared by the intense heat and they cursed the name of God, who had control over these plagues, but they refused to repent and glorify him.'*
>
> (16:9)

The moral effect of God's revelation of himself to the worshippers of the beast is not remedial. Instead of repenting and giving God the glory, they blame him for their suffering. Their wickedness is intensified by the judgment, and their rebellion finds expression in words of blasphemy.

The unrepenting heart is always hardened in sin and becomes more set in enmity against God because of his righteous judgments. It perverts God's revelation and makes it a means of its own hardening (Exodus 7:13-14; John 12:40).

4. The last three bowls (16:10-21)

a. The fifth bowl

> *'The fifth angel poured out his bowl on the throne of the beast, and his kingdom was plunged into darkness. Men gnawed their tongues in agony and cursed the God of heaven because of their pains and their sores, but they refused to repent of what they had done.'*
>
> (16:10-11)

The pouring out of the contents of the fifth bowl upon the 'throne' of world power indicates that the dragon's power at its centre is threatened. The darkness symbolises internal strife, confusion, calamity, disorder, distress and division. It is a condition of gloom; its inhabitants are helpless. When men and women refuse the light offered to them, they forfeit the illumination they need for life and conduct.

b. The sixth bowl

> *'I saw three evil spirits that looked like frogs; they came out of the mouth of the dragon, out of the mouth of the beast and out of the mouth of the false prophet. They are spirits of demons performing miraculous signs, and they go out to the kings of the whole world, to gather them for the battle on the great day of God Almighty.'*
>
> (16:13-14)

John pictures the hosts of evil against which the agents of God enter into conflict. Three 'evil spirits' are seen coming out of the mouths of the dragon (Satan), the beast (world power) and the false prophet (false religion). The fact that the evil spirits come from their mouths symbolises that they are false teachings. The number 'three' is a parody on the holy number of the Trinity. These spirits are foes of Christ and his church.

> *'They gathered the kings together to the place that in Hebrew is called Armageddon.'*
>
> (16:16)

The three frog-like demonic spirits assemble the kings of the whole world to 'Armageddon', a term used symbolically much as we use the term 'Waterloo' today. John uses Armageddon as a symbol of decisive conflict and battle — the struggle of the forces of good against the forces of evil.

John says nothing here about the time of Armageddon. It will occur at no particular time, for it is occurring all the time. The truth which John is seeking to express is timeless and universal. Armageddon has no location on any map of the world.[1] It symbolises the place of defeat for those who take a stand against God and his people.

---

1. William Barclay, *The Revelation of John*, The Daily Study Bible, St Andrew Press, 1959/1976

c. The seventh bowl

> *'The seventh angel poured out his bowl into the air, and out of the temple came a loud voice from the throne, saying, "It is done!" '*
>
> (16:17)

The 'air' is the special sphere and dwelling of Satan, who is 'the ruler of the kingdom of the air' (Ephesians 2:2). Another symbolic meaning of 'air' is the unlimited, in other words, everywhere, every place or every part. John seems to have both ideas in mind. Evil is now being attacked in its own sphere and in all places. 'The last bowl of wrath set the whole of nature at war with man.'[1]

The 'loud voice' which came out of the temple from the throne is the voice of God. God himself says the bowl-plagues are finished. This is the final visitation of his wrath.

Because of a severe earthquake the great city, Babylon, splits into three parts, and the cities of the nations collapse — their ordered society, ranged against God, is ruined (16:18-19). God's purpose is accomplished.

> *'From the sky huge hailstones of about a hundred pounds each fell upon men. And they cursed God on account of the plague of hail, because the plague was so terrible.'*
>
> (16:21)

The whole symbolism is designed to show that the judgment of God is complete. It is a frightful image to denote the terrible and certain destruction which comes upon world power (Babylon). There is no escape from God's judgments.

Study questions on Chapter 6: The Battle and the Bowls

1. In what ways can we be guilty of practising 'false religion' instead of true faith in Jesus? How can we change?

---

1. William Barclay, *The Revelation of John*, The Daily Study Bible, St Andrew Press, 1959/1976

2. 'The object of a man's devotion transforms him into its character'. Consider the reality of this statement in your daily life (see Psalm 115:4-8; 135:15-18).

3. How would you reconcile the apparent paradox that Satan has been defeated yet he is still fighting against the church?

4. Look up Daniel 7. Compare it with what you have learned so far in this study of Revelation. What similarities and differences can you discover?

5. Consider God's command to the Israelites in Deuteronomy 6:6-8 to bind his Word upon their foreheads and hands. In what ways has the Holy Spirit sealed you already with the 'mark' of Jesus? In what ways is God's Word sealed in your mind and heart?

True or False

1. Satan's power ended when he was cast down from heaven.

2. The beast from the sea represents world power trying to rise against Christ and his church.

3. The beast from the earth represents all religion that does not worship Christ.

4. Christians will have to beware of using any article which bears the mark of the beast.

5. The antichrist's name will have letters which, numerically, add up to 666.

6. God's wrath is the disastrous consequence of sins working themselves out on those who have deliberately committed them.

7. The seven bowls in many ways parallel the seven seals and seven trumpets, but with greater intensity.

8. The response of unbelievers who live through the judgments of the first four bowls will be one of repentance and weeping.

9. The trio of Satan, the beast and the false prophet is a parody of the divine Trinity.

10. Armageddon is a geographical place north of Judea where the final conflict between good and evil will be fought.

True or False

1.F 2.T 3.T 4.F 5.F 6.T 7.T 8.F 9.T 10.F

7

The Ultimate Victory

Outline analysis chapters 17 — 22

In this final chapter, our outline analysis deals with the last two sections of the book of Revelation:

☐ The Fall of Babylon and Satan (17 — 20)

☐ Everything Made New (21 — 22)

The Fall of Babylon and Satan

(chapters 17 — 20)

The events of the seventh bowl are elaborated and particularised in chapters 17 — 19. John uses symbols which had acquired a well-defined significance for the Hebrews in the course of their history. Their meaning had been stamped upon the people's consciousness by the prophets of Israel.

1. The great prostitute (17:1-8)

> *'One of the seven angels who had the seven bowls came and said to me, "Come, I will show you the punishment of the great prostitute, who sits on many waters." '*
>
> (17:1)

John is to be shown the judgment of 'the great prostitute' (Jeremiah 51:9). This statement connects the vision that follows with the bowl-judgments. The 'great prostitute' is a parody of the church. Just as the majestic, pure, sun-clothed and star-crowned woman in Revelation 12 symbolises the church, the great prostitute symbolises human society without God (Isaiah 23:15; Nahum 3:4-5).

She epitomises irresponsible power, inhumanity and hatred of all that the church stands for. She is a prostitute because she turns people away from their true loyalty to God and into idolatry. The symbols here represent all that seduces, allures, tempts and draws people from God.

> *'I saw that the woman was drunk with the blood of the saints, the blood of those who bore testimony to Jesus. When I saw her, I was greatly astonished.'*
>
> (17:6)

John is astonished because of the mystery of the seeming defeat of good and victory of evil. He has been invited to look at the *judgment* of the great prostitute — which will take place at the end of this vision (chapters 17 — 18) — but he sees her instead destroying the people of God.

The picture is shocking, unbelievable. How long will God allow it to continue? The angel proceeds to show John the prostitute's fate:

> *'The angel said to me: "Why are you astonished? I will explain to you the mystery of the woman and of the beast she rides, which has the seven heads and ten horns. The beast, which you saw, once was, now is not, and will come up out of the Abyss and go to his destruction." '*
>
> (17:7-8)

John's angel-interpreter explains the mystery. The woman and the beast that carries her form one mystery. To know the one is to know the other. The symbolism of the beast is a parody of the title given to God in 1:4.

> *'The beast who once was, and now is not, is an eighth king. He belongs to the seven and is going to his destruction.'*
>
> (17:11)

The seven kings describe world power as it exists throughout all generations. John says in this mysterious statement that, one after another, the kingdoms of the world will fall; then, last of all, the supernatural power which sustains them will also go to its destruction.

2. War with the Lamb (17:14)

> *'They will make war against the Lamb, but the Lamb will overcome them because he is Lord of lords and King of kings — and with him will be his called, chosen and faithful followers.'*
>
> (17:14)

This war between the Lamb and all the powers of evil extends throughout the history of the world. The beast may exercise dominion and power in the world as 'prince of this world', but the Lamb is still greater. Not only will the Lamb fight and overcome, but those associated with him are permitted to share in the battles and the victory.

John refers to Jesus as the Lamb who engages in the struggle because the victory is won in a *spiritual* warfare (2 Corinthians 10:3-6) totally different from warfare in this world.

> *'The beast and the ten horns you saw will hate the prostitute. They will bring her to ruin and leave her naked; they will eat her flesh and burn her with fire.'*
>
> (17:16)

Here is the fate of false religion. It brings about its own destruction. The world power (the beast with the ten horns), in which she trusts, rises in rebellion and destroys her (Ezekiel 16:35-43; 23:22). False religion is completely destroyed by those whom she seduces and makes drunk with the wine of her fornication. In John's time this was true of the adulterous relationship between Israel and Rome (for example, the Jews using the Romans to crucify Christ and to persecute the early church).

> *'God has put it into their hearts to accomplish his purpose by agreeing to give the beast their power to rule, until God's words are fulfilled. The woman you saw is the great city that rules over the kings of the earth.'*
>
> (17:17-18)

The nations are performing the will of the beast, and yet God is working above all, utilising them as his agents in bringing about his purposes (Habakkuk 1:5-11). In destroying false religion, they think they are accomplishing their own purposes (as did the Assyrians in Isaiah 10), but in fact they are carrying out God's purposes. Both world power and false religion thus go down in ruins. Antichristian forces are doomed, and God is victorious.

Note that the prostitute and Babylon are again said to be identical (17:5).

3. The fall of Babylon (18:1-24)

> *'With a mighty voice he shouted: "Fallen! Fallen is Babylon the Great! She has become a home for demons and a haunt for every evil spirit, a haunt for every unclean and detestable bird." '*
>
> (18:2)

The angel announces with a 'mighty voice' the utter destruction of Babylon, which is to be identified with the prostitute of the preceding chapter. Babylon, presented here as a pretentious, worldly, corrupt and domineering city, symbolises false religion which deceives the whole world and for whom a suprahistorical judgment awaits.

The three phrases used to describe fallen Babylon express the loathsome state to which she is reduced. John draws a picture of utter destruction, emptiness and desolation, the complete ruin which overtakes false religion.

> *'Give back to her as she has given; pay her back double for what she has done. Mix her a double portion from her own cup.'*
>
> (18:6)

The extremity of Babylon's guilt calls for punishment in full measure. The iniquities with which she filled her cup (17:4) have now turned into the wine of the wrath of God. The seeds of judgment lie in every evil principle, and these seeds must germinate and produce fruit when they are planted.

> *'A mighty angel picked up a boulder the size of a large millstone and threw it into the sea, and said: "With such violence the great city of Babylon will be thrown down, never to be found again." '*
>
> (18:21)

In verses 21-24 John gives a dramatic picture of the desolation of Babylon. The destruction of the city is complete, assuring the church, in intense symbolism, that false religion is to be destroyed. Christ is in his church (1:12-20) and he will not forget his promises, nor will his faithfulness fail. God in Christ is pledged to the overthrow of false religion.

The destruction of Babylon is the overthrow by God of all that is false and passing, in order that the true and eternal may take its proper place.

4. The wedding of the Lamb (19:1-10)

After the fall of Babylon a victory song is heard in heaven:

> *'I heard what sounded like the roar of a great multitude in heaven shouting: "Hallelujah! Salvation and glory and power belong to our God, for true and just are his judgments." '*
>
> (19:1-2)

The twenty-four elders and the four living creatures fall down to worship God (19:4) in agreement with this victory song. But there is more to celebrate; now is the time for the wedding of the Lamb:

> *'I heard what sounded like a great multitude, like the roar of rushing waters and like loud peals of thunder, shouting: "Hallelujah! For our Lord God Almighty reigns. Let us rejoice and be glad and give him glory! For the wedding of the Lamb has come, and his bride has made herself ready." '*
>
> (19:6-7)

His bride, the church, is wearing 'fine linen, bright and clean' and this stands for 'the righteous acts of the saints' (19:8). Our preparation for the wedding, therefore, is a life marked by righteous acts. While it remains true that God is sanctifying us through and through (1 Thessalonians 5:23-24), we also have to purify *ourselves* (1 John 3:2-3) in preparation for that day.

5. The fall of the beast and the false prophet (19:11-21)

a. The conquering Christ

> *'I saw heaven standing open and there before me was a white horse, whose rider is called Faithful and True. With justice he judges and makes war.'*
>
> (19:11)

John introduces this vision by saying that he saw 'heaven standing open'. He had insights beyond earthly reasoning, events and circumstances. In the vision he saw a mysterious warrior on a white horse. The white horse is symbolic of victory and the rider is Christ.

The term 'Faithful and True' indicates that he is worthy of the church's confidence. Because he is faithful, he cannot allow his people to struggle alone. Because he is true, he must bring truth to victory.

b. The defeat of the beast and his allies (19:17-21)

> *'I saw an angel standing in the sun, who cried in a loud voice to all the birds flying in mid-air, "Come, gather together for the great supper of God, so that you may eat . . . the flesh of all people, free and slave, small and great." '*
>
> (19:17-18)

An unidentified angel 'standing in the sun', where his voice could be clearly heard, summons the birds of prey to assemble together to feast on the remains of the slain (Ezekiel 39:17-20).

It must be remembered that the battle is a *symbol* of the struggle between good and evil, represented by the total defeat of an army, the bodies of the slain being left unburied on the battlefield. It is a graphic symbolic representation of the utter defeat of all enemies of Christ and the church.

The 'great supper of God' is in grim contrast with the marriage supper of the Lamb (19:9). The feast for the scavenging birds is made from all classes of people. The account indicates the widespread and complete nature of God's judgment, which none will be able to escape.

> *'The rest of them were killed with the sword that came out of the mouth of the rider on the horse, and all the birds gorged themselves on their flesh.'*
>
> (19:21)

John here completes the picture of destruction of the armies opposed to Christ. 'The rest' includes all the antichristian forces described as following the beast and the false prophet (19:18-19). These were slain with the sword coming from the mouth of the rider on the white horse, whose truth is a spiritual weapon of irresistible power (Isaiah 11:4; Daniel 7:11). No rebellion against the King of kings and Lord of lords can prevail.

6. Satan defeated (20:1-15)

In the previous section, the battle has been fought, the two leaders captured and hurled into utter destruction and the vast army of evil destroyed. This army of evil, led by the beast and the false prophet, is really under the direction of the dragon, who alone remains, like a general left behind on a battlefield. He is baffled, deserted and helpless, awaiting sentence by the foes who now surround him.

a. The binding of Satan (20:1-3)

> *'I saw an angel coming down out of heaven, having the key to the Abyss and holding in his hand a great chain.'*
>
> (20:1)

The fact that the angel comes from heaven means that what transpires is not what humankind does but what God accomplishes. The symbols of key and chain express the reduction in the scope of the dragon's power. This curtailment is described under the figure of a strong man bound by an even stronger one (Matthew 12:26, 29; Mark 3:27).

b. The thousand years (20:1-3)

> *'He seized the dragon, that ancient serpent, who is the devil, or Satan, and bound him for a thousand years. He threw him into the Abyss, and locked and sealed it over him, to keep him from deceiving the nations any more until the thousand years were ended. After that, he must be set free for a short time.'*
>
> (20:2-3)

In keeping with John's symbolic use of numbers, we should not see the thousand years as a literal period but as a symbol for a long and complete period of time. 'Since the number ten signifies completeness, and since one thousand is ten to the third power, we may think of the expression "a thousand years" as standing for a complete period, a very long period of indeterminate length.'[1]

This passage, more than any other in Revelation, has provoked wide speculation. But we should remember that this thousand-year period — or 'millennium' — is referred to only in this chapter, suggesting that it has often been credited with disproportionate importance.

Will there be, as some argue, a literal thousand-year period, between this age and the age to come, when Christ and his people will reign in a world without Satan?

In forming a conclusion, it is important to remember that the binding of Satan has *already* taken place (see Matthew 12:29). We are already reigning with Christ, seated with him in the heavenly realms (Ephesians 2:6). Christ himself has all power and authority, and with this in mind commissioned his disciples to 'go and make disciples of *all nations*' (Matthew 28:19).

---

1. Anthony A. Hoekema, *The Bible and the Future*, Eerdmans/Paternoster Press, 1978

Satan is bound or restrained in his ability to *deceive the nations* (Gentiles) the way he did before Pentecost, when God's dealings were almost exclusively with the Jews.

This doesn't mean that Satan is bound in other ways. On the contrary, he will seek to interfere with the outworking of God's purpose in every possible way, but will lack the full power to keep men and women from responding to the truth.

By casting out demons, Jesus proved that his kingdom rule was already here (Matthew 12:28). This is the gospel that we proclaim (Matthew 13:24-30) and which his disciples demonstrated when they returned and exclaimed:

> *'Lord, even the demons submit to us in your name.'*
>
> (Luke 10:17)

They were discovering the reality of the binding of Satan referred to by Jesus when he said, 'I saw Satan fall like lightning from heaven' (Luke 10:18). He meant that by the spiritual action of their faith they were undermining the power of the enemy to deceive, blind or destroy the sons of men (Luke 10:17-18).

Perhaps it is best, then, to conclude that the thousand years symbolises the period extending from the first coming of Christ to just before his return, though this view, like the others, leaves a number of questions unanswered.

c. A vision of thrones (20:4-6)

> *'I saw thrones on which were seated those who had been given authority to judge. And I saw the souls of those who had been beheaded because of their testimony for Jesus and because of the word of God. They had not worshipped the beast or his image and had not received his mark on their foreheads or their hands.'*
>
> (20:4)

i. The souls of the beheaded

'Beheaded' (Greek *pelekizo*) refers to the judicial axe carried by one of the officers or guards before a high Roman magistrate, secured in a bundle of rods (the *fasces*). A corresponding expression today could be 'smitten by the hammer and sickle'.

As such it would not refer to literal martyrs but to martyrs (or witnesses — same word) symbolising disciples in general (see Luke 14:27; Colossians 3:1-3).

ii. The first resurrection

> *'(The rest of the dead did not come to life until the thousand years were ended.) This is the first resurrection.'*
>
> (20:5)

Whether the resurrection spoken of here is spiritual (as in Romans 6:4 and Ephesians 2:4-6) or physical is open to debate. What is clear is that this first resurrection applies only to Christ's people. The 'second death' (eternal death) has no power over them. They are described as priests and kings, reigning with Christ for a thousand years (20:5-6; compare 5:10; 1 Peter 2:9; Romans 5:17). There is also a resurrection for the rest of the dead, after the thousand years (20:5, 11-15).

d. The temporary loosing of Satan (20:7-8)

> *'When the thousand years are over, Satan will be released from his prison.'*
>
> (20:7)

Satan is now allowed a short period of release to try and deceive the nations again (so that they believe the lie of 2 Thessalonians 2:9-12) and to gather his troops.

> *'[Satan] will go out to deceive the nations in the four corners of the earth — Gog and Magog — to gather them for battle. In number they are like the sand on the seashore.'*
>
> (20:8)

In Ezekiel 38 — 39 Gog is a chief prince and Magog is the land over which he ruled (Genesis 10:2). In Ezekiel 38:17-18 the names are symbolic of all the enemies of God's people.

e. The end of the devil (20:9-10)

> *'The devil, who deceived them, was thrown into the lake of burning sulphur, where the beast and the false prophet had been thrown. They will be tormented day and night for ever and ever.'*
>
> (20:10)

At last every vestige of evil is obliterated in the final destruction of the devil himself, who is the embodiment of all evil. John has been building up to this climax, in which the triumph of the kingdom of God is poised for completion.

f. The judgment of all the enemies of Christ (20:11-15)

> *'I saw a great white throne and him who was seated on it. Earth and sky fled from his presence, and there was no place for them.'*
>
> (20:11)

The enemies of Christ and his church have one by one passed from view and have been thrown into the lake of fire. Only people remain to be dealt with, both the redeemed and the unredeemed:

> *'I saw the dead, great and small, standing before the throne, and books were opened. Another book was opened, which is the book of life. The dead were judged according to what they had done as recorded in the books.'*
>
> (20:12)

Here, the finalising of the destinies of men and women is represented under the image of a solemn judicial procedure. The major point of the scene is that none will elude the judgment of God (John 5:28-29; Romans 2:3).

> *'Death and Hades were thrown into the lake of fire. The lake of fire is the second death.'*
>
> (20:14)

John assures the church of the certain destruction of *all* their enemies. Death and the grave no longer have power over the redeemed, who await the new Jerusalem from heaven. All evil has now been destroyed; only God's power remains. This leaves no further obstacle to the establishment of the reign of God in its totality.

Everything Made New

(chapters 21 — 22)

1. A new heaven and a new earth (21:1-8)

While God's judgment is active upon all who oppose Christ and his church, his grace is also generous towards all who accept and follow him. In this vision, John turns from the judgment of evil to the rewarding of the good.

He paints an idealistic picture of the glorious reality of the church as it will be, and of the earth when the church will have accomplished its mission. The triumph of the cause of Christ is complete and eternal:

> *'I saw a new heaven and a new earth, for the first heaven and the first earth had passed away, and there was no longer any sea.'*
>
> (21:1)

John pictures a re-creation of the world. This is his picturesque symbol of a new order demonstrating the renovating power of Christ through the church in the world (Matthew 19:28; John 3:3; Acts 3:20-21). It is the full spiritual restoration which Christ came into the world to promote and which has been proceeding ever since. It is in progress now and will continue from generation to generation until 'the time comes for God to restore everything, as he promised long ago through his holy prophets' (Acts 3:21).

The Greek word for 'new' designates something which already exists but now appears in a new or fresh aspect. It is an already existing heaven and earth now completely transformed:

> *'I heard a loud voice from the throne saying, "Now the dwelling of God is with men, and he will live with them. They will be his people, and God himself will be with them and be their God." '*
>
> (21:3)

God dwells with his church. They are his people and he is with them as their God. In the church, men and women are fully and for ever reconciled to God, whose eternal purpose of dwelling with his people is totally fulfilled.

> *'He who was seated on the throne said, "I am making everything new!" Then he said, "Write this down, for these words are trustworthy and true." '*
>
> (21:5)

John emphasises the fact that it is *God* who is transforming the old into the new. He is on the throne, with the sovereign power to carry on and complete the new creation (4:2). Just as he brought the original creation from chaos to order (Genesis 1), so by his redemptive power God is producing a new moral and spiritual order out of moral chaos.

God commands John to write because the truth of the revelation is accurate. What he has revealed about making a new creation is his own divine purpose, which nothing can thwart. The convulsive struggles of the old order, among which John lives, are merely the birth-pangs of the new creation (Romans 8:22-25).

2. The new Jerusalem (21:9-27)

Earlier, John had been asked to look at the fall of Babylon (17:1-3; 18:1-2). Now he is invited to feast his eyes on God's city, the new Jerusalem.

> *'One of the seven angels who had the seven bowls full of the seven last plagues came and said to me, "Come, I will show you the bride, the wife of the Lamb." And he carried me away in the Spirit to a mountain great and high, and showed me the Holy City, Jerusalem, coming down out of heaven from God. It shone with the glory of God, and its brilliance was like that of a very precious jewel, like a jasper, clear as crystal.'*
>
> (21:9-11)

John isn't picturing a scene in a distant heaven somewhere in space. He is recording a vision of the church on earth, 'the bride, the wife of the Lamb'. Nor is he concerned with a place or building, but a *people*, employing physical objects to represent spiritual realities.

The church he describes is an ideal church. It isn't to be separated from the final dwelling of the redeemed. It now exists, but its perfected splendour will appear only in the age to come. The heavenly begins on earth, and this is a vision of the heavenly on earth (Ephesians 1:3, 19-20; 2:6-7; Philippians 3:20-21). It is a vision of all the redeemed of God in the life of the Spirit that transcends the limitations of time and place.

> *'The angel who talked with me had a measuring rod of gold to measure the city, its gates and its wall. The city was laid out like a square, as long as it was wide. He measured the city with the rod and found it to be 12,000 stadia in length, and as wide and high as it is long.'*
>
> (21:15-16)

The symbolism of the measuring of the Holy City comes from Ezekiel 40 — 43. By this symbolism John intends to show that the whole city, like the temple Holy of Holies, is the dwelling-place of God. Previously, John himself had been told to 'measure the temple' (11:1); here the skill of an angel is needed for this greater task. The act of measuring emphasises the city's greatness, symmetry, solidity and splendour. The cube (four-square) symbolises permanence and perfection (Exodus 39:8-9). The Holy of Holies in Solomon's temple was a perfect cube (1 Kings 6:19-20).

3. Life and light in the Holy City (22:1-5)

> *'The angel showed me the river of the water of life, as clear as crystal, flowing from the throne of God and of the Lamb down the middle of the great street of the city. On each side of the river stood the tree of life, bearing twelve crops of fruit, yielding its fruit every month. And the leaves of the tree are for the healing of the nations.'*
>
> (22:1-2)

The first five verses of this chapter conclude John's description of the Holy City. His picture of the interior of the city (Psalm 46:4) is one of perfect peace. It is a garden city where all is in order, where a river runs, where flowers and fruit of refreshment and healing abound. The water of the river is sufficient for all needs.

John is saying that the redeemed have entered upon a full, meaningful and abundant life which will be theirs for ever. Their spiritual life here is but the imperfect stage of the life to come (John 5:24; 6:47). The gift of the Spirit is the guarantee of their inheritance (2 Corinthians 5:5). In the Holy City they have been translated into the life-state which is the 'eternal now'.

> *'No longer will there be any curse. The throne of God and of the Lamb will be in the city, and his servants will serve him. They will see his face, and his name will be on their foreheads. There will be no more night. They will not need the light of a lamp or the light of the sun, for the Lord God will give them light. And they will reign for ever and ever.'*
>
> (22:3-5)

In these verses John reiterates his description of the church. The curse, the element of disorder in the moral sphere, is removed. God and the Lamb rule jointly.

Formerly, it was the special privilege of the high priest alone to enter the Holy of Holies to meet God, and that only one day in a year. Now, it is the privilege of the whole redeemed community to be in God's presence continuously, to serve him and to reign with him for ever.

There is an intimacy to be constantly enjoyed between God and humankind which was previously impossible. All the barriers between them have been removed. God's authority is everywhere recognised, and his servants serve him. Everything is seen through him, and everything is done for him. Life is flooded with light; darkness of every kind is banished for ever. The church shares in the reign of Christ and, in their doing so, the goal and essence of true life is realised.

4. Conclusion (22:6-21)

> *'I warn everyone who hears the words of the prophecy of this book: If anyone adds anything to them, God will add to him the plagues described in*

this book. And if anyone takes words away from this book of prophecy, God will take away from him his share in the tree of life and in the holy city, which are described in this book. He who testifies to these things says, "Yes, I am coming soon." Amen. Come, Lord Jesus. The grace of the Lord Jesus be with God's people. Amen.'

(22:18-21)

The epilogue confirms and underscores the visions seen by John. It is personal and direct, containing short sayings, practical exhortations, promises, assurances, blessings and warnings, each repeating some phrase which has gone before. Together, they show how the purpose set forth at the beginning has been carried out.

We conclude with a quotation from William Hendriksen which summarises the closing verses:

'Because this book of Revelation is so transcendentally glorious, so divine, for God himself is the author, let no-one who hears or reads this book add or subtract a word. Let him not call this writing spurious. Let him not say that its meaningful passages are interpolations. Let him not deny its divinely inspired character. Let him not say that it is hardly worth studying. Let him not ridicule this book, filled with invitations and promises. If he refuses to heed this warning, the plagues written in this book will be added to him. God will take away his part from the tree of life and the Holy City.

'Christ answers the ardent prayer of the church for his coming by saying: "Yes, I am coming soon." Let us, therefore, heed his warnings. John's heart is filled with rapture. His soul is consumed with longing. His eye attempts to pierce the clouds. In an ecstasy of love, he exclaims, "Amen. Come, Lord Jesus." '[2]

2. William Hendriksen, *More Than Conquerors — An Interpretation of the Book of Revelation*, Baker Book House/Tyndale Press, 1939/1967

Study questions on Chapter 7: The Ultimate Victory

1. John describes the church as the new Holy City. What is in store for the church, according to Revelation 21:9-11?

2. What are your thoughts and feelings about what the completed kingdom of God will be like? What are some of the great things God has already provided for us, as well as what he has in store for us in the age to come?

3. Meditate on the truth that you are the dwelling-place of God. Make a list of what that says about your identity.

4. Consider the last statements of John in Revelation. Do you handle the Word of God as reverently as he commands? How can your personal study of God's Word help you gain wisdom, inspiration and admonition from the Lord?

True or False

1. The great prostitute symbolises human society without God.

2. False religion will develop the elements of its own destruction.

3. Babylon represents the large cities in our society which are full of evil and wickedness.

4. Evil is defeated when the church goes forth to combat with Christ leading them.

5. It is the church that will rise up and cast Satan into the Abyss for ever and ever.

6. The binding of Satan has already taken place.

7. The redeemed of the Lord will be resurrected on the Last Day, but the unredeemed will remain in death.

8. By his redemptive power, God is producing a new moral and spiritual order out of moral chaos.

9. God's eternal purpose is to dwell with his people.

True or False

1.T 2.T 3.F 4.T 5.F 6.T 7.F 8.T 9.T